Pattern Design for Needlepoint & Patchwork

Pattern Design for Needlepoint & Patchwork

By Susan Schoenfeld

with Winifred Bendiner

 Van Nostrand Reinhold Company
New York Cincinnati Toronto London Melbourne

Acknowledgments

First, I would like to thank my husband, Howard Kalish, who took all photographs that appear in this book (except for Color Plates 32 and 13 and Figs. 183, 194, and 208, which were taken by David Moy), and who helped me to organize and execute all the drawings, who learned to do needlepoint, and without whose constant help and hard work this book could not have been completed.

The following people also richly deserve my thanks for their contributions:

Elinor and Nancy Migdal and Doris Gluck, and the many other friends and students whose enthusiasm and willingness to work untried patterns helped me to clarify the needlepoint methods which are given here.

My mother, Lillian Schoenfeld, whose interest in crafts and textiles started me on the path which led to the writing of this book.

Ben and Marcia Schonzeit, for allowing us to use their studio and equipment to take the photographs.

And a special thanks to Barbara Klinger, the editor of this book, for her coherency and good advice in the organization and presentation of this material.

Van Nostrand Reinhold Company Regional Offices:
New York Cincinnati Chicago Millbrae Dallas
Van Nostrand Reinhold Company International Offices:
London Toronto Melbourne

Library of Congress Catalog Card Number 72-9709
ISBN 0-442-27417-3

All drawings by Susan Schoenfeld; all photographs by Howard
Kalish, except Color Plates 32 and 13, Figs. 183, 194, and 208 (by
David Moy), and where otherwise credited.
Designed by Rosa Delia Vasquez

V.I.P. typeset and printed in Great Britain by
Jolly & Barber Ltd., Rugby.

Published by Van Nostrand Reinhold Company
A Division of Litton Educational Publishing, Inc.
450 West 33rd Street, New York, N.Y. 10001
Published simultaneously in Canada by
Van Nostrand Reinhold Company Ltd.

16 15 14 13 12 11 10 9 8 7 6 5 4 3 2 1

Contents

Preface   7

1. Introduction   9

2. Materials & Stitches   16

3. Choosing & Coloring Your Design   28

4. Transferring the Design   31

5. Pattern Sheet I: The Even-Numbered Square   40

6. Pattern Sheet II: The Odd-Numbered Square   64

7. Pattern Sheet III: The Equilateral Triangle   104

8. Pattern Sheet IV: The Circle   132

9. Finishing Your Needlepoint   165

10. Patchwork & Appliqué   170

11. Designing Your Own Pattern   196

This example of Japanese lacquer work from the nineteenth century contains various geometric patterns that can be translated into needlepoint or patchwork designs. (The Metropolitan Museum of Art, Rogers Fund, 1913.)

Preface

Until recently, for no intrinsic reason other than custom, the craft of needlepoint has been closely identified with what might be loosely termed the "needlepoint style." This style, featuring flowery patterns designed to cover baroque chairs and the like, is well-known to all and well-loved by many (including myself), but it is one which I have found hard to fit into my home and into my life-style. I have always loved to sew, to crochet and embroider; but I wanted to make needlepoint pillows and rugs, upholstery and handbags, that fit a more contemporary sense of design.

For me (and I think also for many others, as history proves), the most useful designs are geometric. Geometric designs are probably the most logical, well-balanced, and universal of all forms of pattern design; accordingly they fit most easily into any surroundings. (You can confirm this by looking around at this very moment; chances are you will see not one, but many geometric designs.)

Although geometric designs have previously been excluded from the purview of needlepoint, in recent years, the field of needlepoint has opened up, admitting more and more diverse designs and including many more different styles. The barrier of habit no longer prevented my working non-traditional designs in needlepoint. The only barriers which did exist, I found, were those within the materials themselves.

I began by adapting those geometric designs I was fondest of into needlepoint pieces. I didn't limit myself to needlepoint patterns, but rather ranged over the whole world of design, researching historical examples and picking a mosaic-tile pattern from one place, a parquet-floor design from another.

It soon became apparent that, buried within these designs, was something common to them all; a basic geometric structure. And this provided the means for systematically adapting geometric designs to needlepoint.

To a person with a systematic turn of mind—which I must confess I am, a system can be a very beautiful thing. Having discovered one of my own, I felt it was well worth going out of my way to pursue. So I did further research, and read books on the principles of geometric design. I graphed out endless patterns, and sent for more to far-flung museums. In working the designs on canvas, I discovered the relationships between the patterns and the ways of executing the stitches. The results of my discoveries is what follows—a book about geometric pattern design and needlecraft.

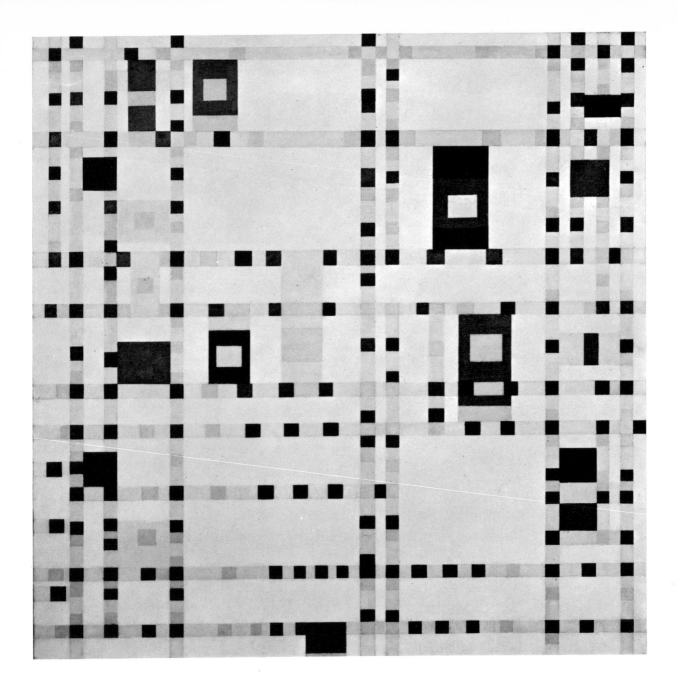

Though it might seem that a geometric pattern made up of nothing but horizontal and vertical lines has limited potential, this beautiful painting by Piet Mondrian, called *Broadway Boogie-Woogie,* shows what can be done by a master artist. (Oil on canvas, 50 by 50 inches; 1942-43; Collection, The Museum of Modern Art, New York.)

1. Introduction

It may seem to some that geometry and needlecraft have only a nodding acquaintance with each other—as, for instance, mathematics and cooking—but this is far from the truth. Geometric design and needlecraft are in fact intimately related—even closer than cousins; and the relationship began far back in history.

Before such a thing as cloth fabric existed (and cloth is, of course, the basis of all needlecraft), people discovered that they could weave reeds over and under each other to make a unit far stronger and more resilient than any other made from the same materials, and that this durable construction could be used in forming a basket or a mat (Fig. 1). Gradually, through history, the fibrous material that was used for weaving became more and more refined, thinner and thinner—until it was only a thread. But the principle of construction remained the same: the weaving of strands of equal thickness at right angles.

There were other methods of weaving baskets, with the reeds at other than right angles, and today there are many different ways of interlacing threads to form fabrics, but it was this basic basket weave which became the foundation for making cloth. And, if one were to look closely at most woven cloth today, the construction would look like the representation in Fig. 2. Some fabrics might be woven more closely, some less; the threads might be thinner or thicker; but in principle the majority of the weaves would be similar to the primitive basket weave.

The reason for the preponderancy of this method of making cloth is the resulting strength, resiliency, and simplicity. But the cloth has another property as well, which is neither incidental nor accidental: it is perfectly geometric. The warp and the weft of such fabrics make hundreds and thousands of tiny little squares. The canvas that is used for needlepoint is simply loosely woven fabric in which the squares are more apparent.

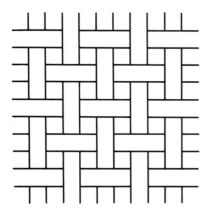

Fig. 1. Basket weaving has an inherent geometric construction.

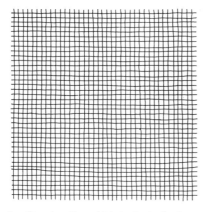

Fig. 2. Construction of fabrics is similar to woven reeds.

This geometric quality was inherent in the weaving process, so that weaving with reeds led not only to weaving with threads but to geometric pattern-design as well. The weavers found a natural beauty in the squares formed by the woven reeds and they intuitively began to vary the structural elements in a search for even greater beauty. Sometimes the pattern was varied by changing the color of the reeds (Figs. 3 and 4); sometimes, by changing the size of the reeds (Fig. 5); and sometimes, by adding new reeds (Fig. 6). The variations shown here are but four of the literally thousands of basket-weaving patterns.

Soon other craftsmen began to copy these patterns in other materials, carving them in wood or stone, or painting them on flat surfaces, so that the designs, which in basket weaving grew organically out of the process, became purely decorative. In order to transfer the patterns to other materials, the craftsmen had to re-create the regularity of the woven units on an unwoven surface. The means they found to do this was to first draw a regular linear pattern (Fig. 7) on the surface they intended to decorate.

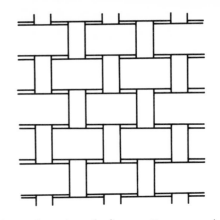

Fig. 5. Sometimes the linear pattern was varied by weaving with reeds of different thicknesses.

Fig. 3. Weavers sometimes varied the basic pattern by using different-colored reeds.

Fig. 6. Another variation was to add diagonal strands.

Fig. 4. Another variation was to paint the woven surface, using the intervals of the weave itself as a basis for creating a regular geometric pattern.

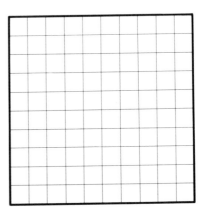

Fig. 7. A drawn linear pattern re-creates the regularity of woven units on an unwoven surface.

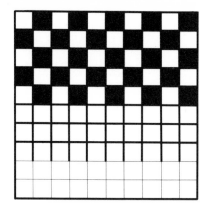

Fig. 8. A simple checkerboard pattern is made by filling in alternate squares created by the linear pattern.

Having drawn the linear structure, they could easily locate the elements of the original, woven design and copy these elements in the proper proportions and at the proper intervals. As time went by, the woven models were dispensed with, and designs were derived from the linear structure itself.

To illustrate how designs may be derived from a purely linear guideline, Figs. 8, 9, 10 and 11 show how each of four different designs comes from one underlying structure. The lines form a pattern of equal-size squares. Each small square is one unit of the pattern, and each of these may be divided into smaller, triangular units by diagonal lines. All of these units are design elements. The variety in the designs comes from the way the units, or elements, are combined and arranged.

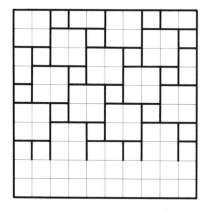

Fig. 9. The same linear structure can create a pattern that alternates large squares with smaller squares (see pattern I-1).

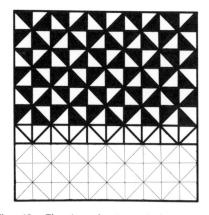

Fig. 10. The introduction of diagonal lines creates a new pattern (see pattern I-5).

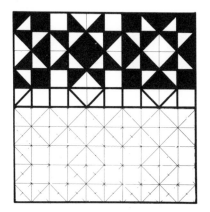

Fig. 11. Combining various diagonals with squares yields this eight-pointed star (see pattern I-9).

For instance, the design in Fig. 10 is accomplished by repeating the arrangement of eight triangular elements shown in Fig. 12. The diagonals of four basic-unit squares are stressed to form the eight triangular elements. The same sequence of elements could be repeated to form a band design or a border design as well (Fig. 13).

By stressing a different diagonal on only two of the four squares in Fig. 12, we can change the pattern completely, although it is still composed of eight triangular elements (Fig. 14). This new sequence of elements can also be repeated to form either a square design, a band, or a border. Such a pattern can be extended endlessly in any direction simply by repeating its arrangement of elements as much as is desired.

You can see the importance of uniformity of line here, a uniformity which does not vary from one unit to the next. It is this very uniformity which gives us the freedom to change the designs. Because they are identical, we can use the units as building blocks.

Fig. 12.   The diagonals of four basic squares are stressed to form eight triangular elements.

Fig. 14.   Although still composed of eight triangular elements, this design differs in the diagonals that are stressed.

Fig. 13.   By repeating the same sequence of elements, we can form a band design or a border design as well as the overall one shown in Fig. 10.

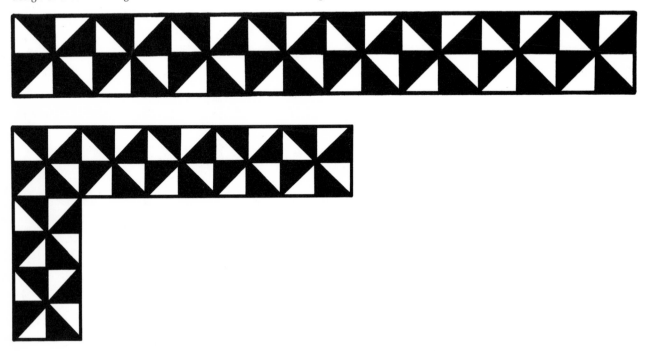

As another example, the eight-pointed star in Fig. 11 is formed from a grouping, or sequence, of units that extends over sixteen squares instead of four. Here the triangular units are combined with square ones as detailed in Fig. 15.

The underlying geometric structure is apparent in these designs and this will be true for all the designs in this book. The structure of squares and diagonals shown here is in fact the basis for all the designs in Chapters 5 and 6. To get an inkling of how many designs can be derived from just the square and the right-angled triangles formed by its diagonals, the reader need only leaf through those two chapters and note that the shapes include rectangles, diamonds, octagons, and chevrons, as well as squares and triangles.

Just as the square is the root shape for the designs in Chapters 5 and 6, the equilateral triangle and the circle are the root shapes for the designs in Chapters 7 and 8. Each root shape forms a uniform, linear network and an underlying structure for separate designs. The designs in Chapter 7, which are based on the equilateral triangle, include such diverse shapes as the hexagon, diamond, and six-pointed star; the designs in Chapter 8, which are based on the circle, include such forms as scallops, leaf-shapes, and floral patterns, among others.

The system of building designs from a basic, uniform structure has been used by artisans and craftsmen, architects and artists, since before the beginning of recorded history. There is a compelling reason for its use: it makes the construction of beautiful, well-proportioned, and endlessly varied designs relatively easy. The system has been applied throughout history to the decoration of buildings, furniture, textiles, clothing, rugs, sculpture, painting, utensils, floors, windows, doors, and almost anything else you would care to mention, including the human body itself (tattooing of aboriginal peoples). It has never gone out of style, and it wouldn't be overventuresome to suggest that it never will.

Fig. 15. The grouping of triangular and square elements that form this eight-pointed star extends over sixteen basic squares rather than four.

Many of the designs in this book, both contemporary and historically documented ones, have in fact been adapted from other media, such as mosaics. In order to simplify their use in needlepoint and patchwork, I have codified the designs so that each one in this book is based on any one of four underlying structures that I have found compatible with needlework. As shown in Fig. 16, the underlying structure of each design is depicted in light lines, while the design itself is drawn in heavy lines superimposed over the light ones. The heavy lines, therefore, show not only the final design, but also how the units and elements of the underlying structure are combined to form it.

In addition, as the line drawings show the designs in a reduced size, each of the four underlying structures has been reproduced as a full-scale pattern sheet (see Fig. 17) whose units correspond exactly to the lighter lines in the drawn design. These pattern sheets, enclosed in an envelope at the back of the book, make it possible to enlarge any of the designs and accurately transfer it to canvas or fabric.

The simple steps of using a pattern sheet to produce a full-scale drawing of the design and of transferring the drawing to canvas will be detailed in later chapters. First, however, I would like to discuss the needlepoint materials and stitches that I have found the most appropriate for this venture in geometric design.

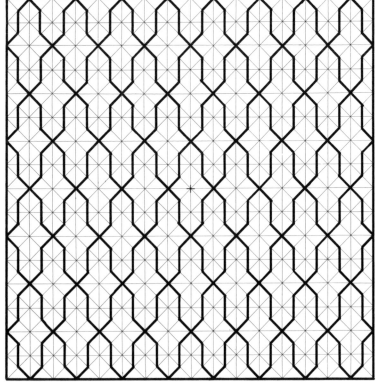

Fig. 16.   Each design in the book is presented as a line drawing. The light lines show the basic underlying structure on which the pattern is based and the heavy lines show how the elements are stressed to form the particular pattern. (This is pattern II-2.)

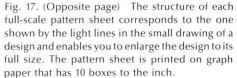

Fig. 17. (Opposite page)   The structure of each full-scale pattern sheet corresponds to the one shown by the light lines in the small drawing of a design and enables you to enlarge the design to its full size. The pattern sheet is printed on graph paper that has 10 boxes to the inch.

2. Materials & Stitches

Canvas

Canvas is a netlike fabric of evenly spaced horizontal and vertical threads woven to produce mesh openings between the threads. The design is usually worked in basic tent stitches by drawing a yarn-threaded needle in and out of diagonally opposite mesh openings so that one intersection of horizontal and vertical threads is covered by one stitch (Fig. 18). This is true whether the canvas is woven with single threads in each direction (mono-canvas, Fig. 19) or with pairs of threads in each direction (penelope canvas, Fig. 20), although there are many additional, decorative stitches that can be used to cover a greater number of intersections at one time or to cover only the horizontal threads instead.

For our purposes, it is preferred that the intersections of the canvas threads be immobile. While penelope canvas is constructed so that the threads are automatically locked in position, mono-canvas sometimes is not, and it is best to specify "locked" canvas when buying mono.

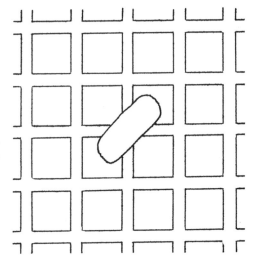

Fig. 18. The basic tent stitch covers one intersection of canvas and always slants in this direction.

Fig. 19. Mono-canvas is woven with single threads in each direction.

Fig. 20. Penelope canvas has pairs of threads in each direction.

The color of the canvas is also a factor. White is recommended because it is easier to see for purposes of marking and counting. Mono-canvas has traditionally been white, but penelope canvas, which has traditionally been tan, is now becoming available in white.

The size or gauge of any needlepoint canvas is denoted by the number of tent stitches per inch it yields. This can vary from 5 stitches per inch to 16. For example, on a No. 10 canvas, 10 tent stitches will cover 10 thread intersections and measure one inch. I recommend using this size canvas because it corresponds in size to the 10-boxes-to-the-inch graph paper on which the full-scale pattern sheets are printed; a needlepoint design worked on No. 10 canvas will therefore be the exact size indicated by the pattern sheet.

Each box on the graph paper of the pattern sheet always stands for one intersection of threads on the canvas and therefore for one tent stitch. Thus if a design unit is 10 graph boxes wide on the pattern sheet, it will invariably be 10 stitches wide on the canvas. If you use a No. 10 canvas, the 10 stitches will extend to a width of one inch, the same width as the 10 boxes on the pattern sheet. If you use a No. 12 canvas, however, which requires 12 stitches to the inch, the 10 stitches will extend to less than one inch, and the needlepoint design will be smaller than the size indicated on the pattern sheet. Similarly, if you use a No. 7 or No. 5 canvas, both of which require fewer than 10 stitches to the inch, the 10 stitches will extend for more than one inch and the finished design will be larger. For this reason, I suggest that you use No. 10 canvas for your first projects taken from this book.

The indicated dimensions of most of the designs will be 16 by 16 inches. Should you wish to extend any design, or to work on a different size canvas, you can calculate the perimeter dimensions of the design on the canvas by dividing the number of stitches required for the outside row by the gauge number of your canvas. For example, if the pattern sheet indicates the design will be 160 stitches in width and you wish to extend it by 20 stitches on No. 10 canvas, divide the 180 stitches by 10 and you get 18 inches. If you wish to do a design measuring 160 stitches across on No. 12 canvas, divide 160 by 12 and you get 13⅓ inches.

Yarn and Needles

Another important factor in working needlepoint designs is to make certain the yarn you use covers the canvas threads completely so no bare threads or mesh openings peek through. I recommend using tapestry yarn for No. 10 penelope canvas and three-stranded Persian wool for No. 10 mono-canvas. You can also use tapestry yarn on No. 10 mono if you take care not to pull the wool too taut. For No. 14 mono-canvas, remove one of the three strands from the Persian wool and use the remaining two strands together. You can do the same for a No. 12 canvas if you make sure the two strands are thick enough to cover the threads properly. Dark colors tend to be less full and do not cover the canvas as well as light colors do. To compensate for this, you can pull the yarn less tightly when using dark colors.

Cotton thread can also be used for needlepoint, but it does not wear as well as wool, and it is not recommended for work which will receive constant use. Persian wool is often sold in ready-cut lengths of about 24 inches; tapestry yarn is sold in skeins which have to be cut into separate lengths. Do not use strands longer than 24 inches or the yarn will fray.

Tapestry needles, which have blunt, rounded ends, are used to work the yarn in and out of the mesh openings. As the eye is large, these needles are easily threaded with yarn. They come in different sizes, but a No. 18 needle works well on No. 10, 12, or 14 canvas.

Using Basic Needlepoint Stitches

The most commonly used stitches in needlepoint are those which come under the general heading of "tent" stitches. These are flat, even stitches which cover one intersection of the threads at a time as previously described.

A tent stitch is the smallest unit in needlepoint. Each stitch always slants in the direction pictured in Fig. 18 (from the lower-left mesh to the upper-right mesh) and each stitch always looks identical to every other stitch, so that, when finished, the work has a tapestry-like appearance.

The stitches that cover more than one intersection of the threads are usually raised and decorative. That being the case, they not only create the problem of fitting evenly within the outlines of a pre-drawn design, they usually create a pattern of their own, which, in many cases, may oppose the patterns of the designs given here. Therefore, I recommend that you use tent stitches for the working of these designs. They are the single-unit "building blocks" for the realization of these designs in needlepoint, just as the root shapes are the building blocks for the designs themselves.

If you do experiment with other stitches, count the number of intersections they cover to make sure that they will fit evenly within the bounds of the area to be filled in. In addition, try to determine that the pattern formed by the stitches and that formed by the design itself are compatible.

Although tent stitches always look identical on the face of the work, they can be made in different ways, according to needle position and sequence. The resulting stitches fall into different categories, each one of which produces its own identifiable pattern on the *back* of the canvas, and each one of which is best for working a particular kind of line or area present in these designs.

There are five tent stitches that I recommend for these designs; four of them are for making single lines of stitching in the four basic directions: horizontal, vertical, lower-right-to-upper-left diagonal, and upper-right-to-lower-left diagonal. The continental stitch is used for working *horizontal* lines, and a vertical variation of the continental stitch is used for *vertical* lines. The diagonal tent stitch is used for *lower-right-to-upper-left diagonal* lines, and the backstitch is used for *upper-right-to-lower-left diagonal* lines. Wherever straight lines of stitches outlining the design elements are called for, these stitches are to be used.

The outlines may then be filled in with the fifth stitch described in this chapter, the ubiquitous and very useful basket weave stitch. The few nooks and crannies into which this stitch does not fit are completed with single tent stitches. The designs given in Chapter 5 are based on pattern sheet I and do not require any outlining stitches; in those cases, the basket weave stitch alone is used with different-colored yarns to fill each area of the design.

Although the movements of the needle in making these five stitches vary, one general common-sense principle applies to all tent stitches, and an understanding of this principle will make the working of these stitches easier. As the stitches must always have the identical slant, each stitch is *always* made with the needle emerging from the lower-left mesh of the intersection to be covered, so it can be inserted in the upper-right mesh of the same intersection. Therefore, you will always want your needle to come out below, and directly to the left of, the next intersection of threads to be covered (Fig. 21). When in doubt, always ask yourself, "Where does the next stitch go?" The stitch you are working on should always end up with the needle in position to make the next stitch.

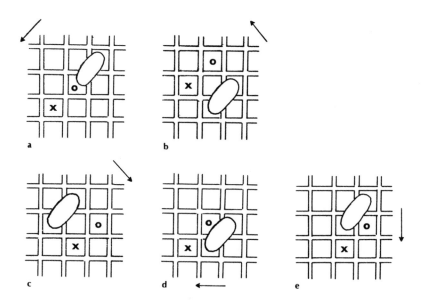

Fig. 21. In working any tent stitch, the needle should always come out below and directly to the left of the next intersection to be covered. In these drawings, **x** shows where the needle should be drawn out to make the next stitch; **o** shows where the needle will be inserted to make that stitch. The arrow shows the direction in which the row is being worked.
(a) backstitch: diagonal row down the canvas
(b) diagonal tent and basket weave: diagonal row up the canvas
(c) basket weave: diagonal row down the canvas
(d) continental: horizontal row
(e) vertical variation: vertical row

The Continental Stitch and Vertical Variation

The continental stitch (Fig. 22) is used for outlining horizontal lines and where only a small area is to be filled in. It is not recommended for large areas of fill-in because it tends to pull the canvas out of shape. Always work in a horizontal row *from right to left*. If it becomes necessary to go from left to right, simply turn the canvas upside down.

A variation of the continental stitch allows you to sew a single row vertically (Fig. 23). Always work the vertical row *down* the canvas. If it becomes necessary to sew up, simply turn the work upside down.

When turning the work, always turn it completely upside down (a full 180°), never halfway, or the stitches will no longer slant in the proper direction.

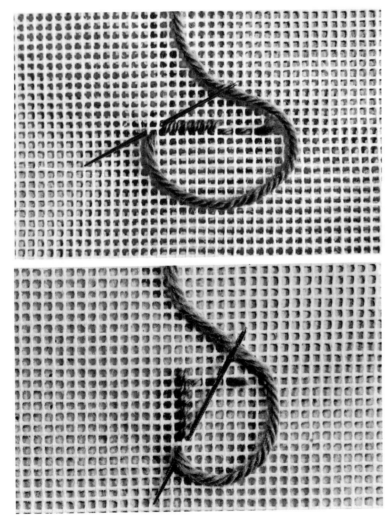

Fig. 22.   Always work the continental stitch from right to left.

Fig. 23.   Always work the vertical variation down the canvas.

The Diagonal Tent Stitch and the Backstitch

The diagonal tent stitch is used for sewing a single row on the lower-right-to-upper-left diagonal (Fig. 24). Work the stitches *up* the canvas as shown. (You may work this diagonal down the canvas only by changing the needle movements as described for the basket weave stitch.)

Because of its own slant, the tent stitch has an especially open appearance when worked on this particular diagonal. However, all spaces between the stitches will be filled by subsequent rows of stitches.

In order to sew a diagonal line in the opposite direction, an upper-right-to-lower-left diagonal, and maintain the proper slant for each tent stitch, it is necessary to change the needle movements to those of the backstitch (Fig. 25). Work these stitches *down* the canvas. In this case, the tent stitches form a continuous line similar to those formed by the continental and vertical variation stitches.

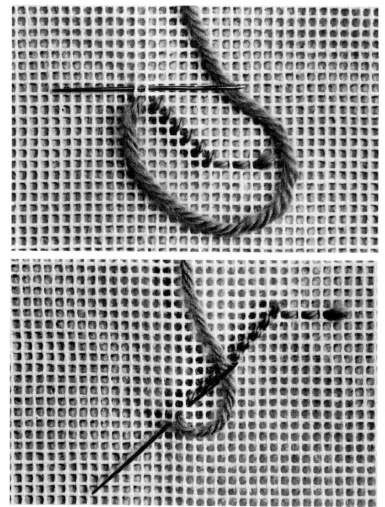

Fig. 24. The diagonal tent stitch up the canvas is used to work the lower-right-to-upper-left diagonal.

Fig. 25. The backstitch is worked down the canvas and forms the upper-right-to-lower-left diagonal.

The Basket Weave Stitch

This stitch is used for filling in areas. It is least apt to pull the canvas out of shape, making blocking easier, and it doesn't necessitate constant turning of the work. Also, it conforms naturally to geometric designs. Since the basket weave stitch is the one used most often, it will benefit beginners to follow these instructions carefully, and to practice the stitch on a small piece of canvas.

The basket weave stitch is made by stitching adjacent diagonal rows, working up one row, then down the row directly to the left, then up the row to the left of that, and so on (Figs. 26 to 37). Each new row is always worked to the left of the previous one. The stitches of each subsequent row interlock with those of the previous row.

As you can see in the series of photographs, the needle is held in a horizontal position when working a diagonal row up the canvas and in a

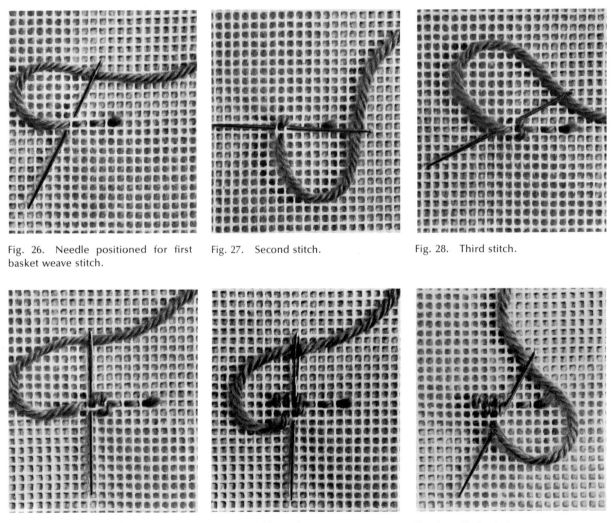

Fig. 26. Needle positioned for first basket weave stitch.

Fig. 27. Second stitch.

Fig. 28. Third stitch.

Fig. 29. Fourth stitch.

Fig. 30. Fifth stitch.

Fig. 31. Sixth stitch.

vertical position when working down the canvas. The only exception is the last stitch of each diagonal row, for which the needle is held in a diagonal position in order to emerge in the proper place for the first stitch of the next row.

Note that the rows worked up the canvas are worked in the same way as the single diagonal row done with the diagonal tent stitch. You could, therefore, begin the basket weave with a single diagonal row worked up the canvas (as in Fig. 24) and continue by working the adjacent diagonal rows up and down the canvas until the desired shape is filled in (see Fig. 39). The stitching sequence used for working a diagonal row down the canvas, with the needle in a vertical position, can be used to work a single row down the canvas (in place of the diagonal tent stitch) if desired.

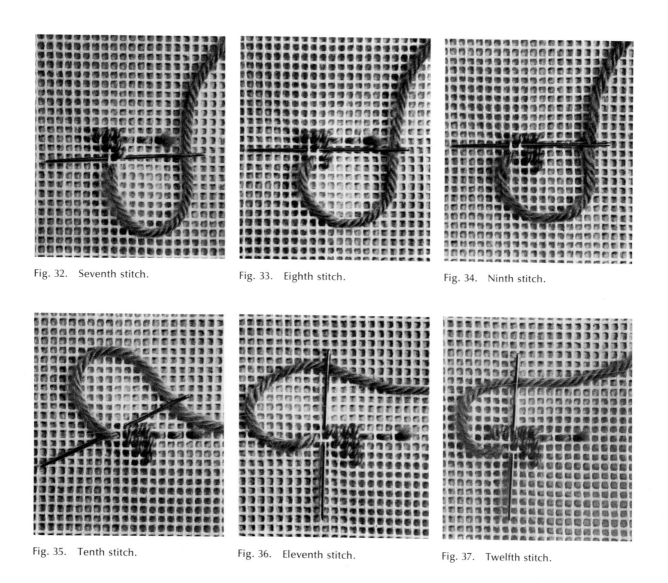

Fig. 32. Seventh stitch.

Fig. 33. Eighth stitch.

Fig. 34. Ninth stitch.

Fig. 35. Tenth stitch.

Fig. 36. Eleventh stitch.

Fig. 37. Twelfth stitch.

By starting in the upper-right corner of the area to be filled, the stitches can be worked as shown in the photographs to fill any shape that includes a right angle in its upper-right corner, such as a square or rectangle, or one of the right triangles formed by the lower-right-to-upper-left diagonal (Fig. 38). The same sequence can be used to fill the bottom triangle formed by that diagonal by turning the canvas upside down to work the stitches. By starting with the diagonal tent stitch, the basket weave can be worked to fill other shapes formed by that diagonal, such as parallelograms, which do not include a right angle (Fig. 39). In addition, by starting as shown in Fig. 40, the basket weave can be used to fill in the two right triangles, or a parallelogram, formed by the lower-left-to-upper-right diagonal. These are just a few examples of how the versatile basket weave can be fitted into geometric shapes. With some exceptions, a general rule to follow is to start at the highest point on the right-hand side of the shape.

Working diagonal rows according to these stitch sequences gives the reverse side of the canvas a woven appearance, from which the stitch takes its name (Fig. 41). The stitches on the reverse side are alternately horizontal and vertical, a result of the position the needle is held in. It is best not to sew two adjacent rows in the same direction. If you end your yarn at the end of a row, remember to begin the next row in the opposite direction. You can tell in which direction the last row was sewn by glancing at the back of the work. A row worked up the diagonal will have horizontal stitches on the reverse side; one worked down the diagonal will have vertical stitches on the back.

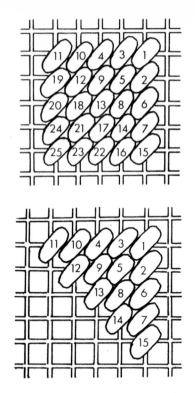

Fig. 38. Basket weave begun in the upper-right corner as in the photographs can be worked to fill these shapes. Sequence of stitches forms diagonal rows up and down the canvas.

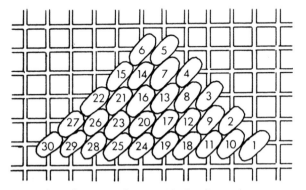

Fig. 39. Basket weave begun with the diagonal tent stitch fills shapes that do not include a right angle.

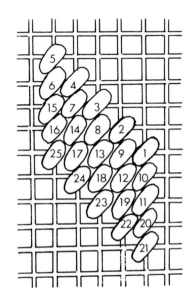

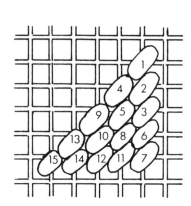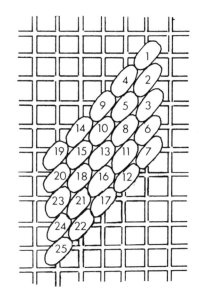

Fig. 40. The starting sequence for working shapes on the upper-right-to-lower-left diagonal.

Fig. 41. Reverse side of canvas shows woven appearance resulting from the basket weave stitch sequence.

Starting and Ending

Never knot the yarn to hold it in place on the canvas. Start a length of yarn by weaving it in and out of alternate mesh openings on a horizontal line just outside the area to be worked, so that you come out directly below and to the left of the intersection that is to hold the first stitch. Fig. 42 shows how the yarn was woven in before the first stitch; the needle followed the same path through the mesh now occupied by the yarn.

Generally speaking, you will use this starting procedure in the very beginning only. Then, as the work progresses, all further startings and endings will be done by weaving the end of the yarn in and out of yarn already in place on the back of the canvas. Begin weaving in the new length about five stitches away in a horizontal or vertical direction from the place you want your needle to emerge, and bring the needle out in position for the next stitch. Leave no more than ⅛-inch of the yarn end showing beyond the first stitch woven through. When ending a length of yarn, weave it through horizontally or vertically for about five stitches on the back of the canvas and then cut the yarn so only about ⅛ of an inch emerges from the last stitch woven through.

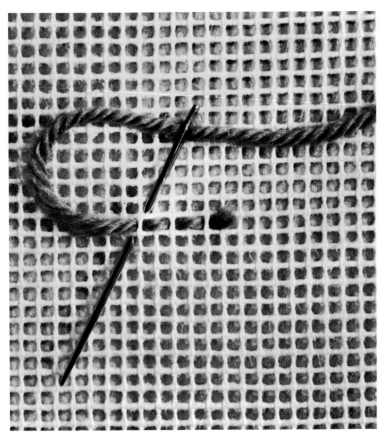

Fig. 42. Yarn is woven in and out of the mesh to hold it in place; it is never knotted.

Sewing Suggestions

In all cases work the wool gently, allowing it to rest on, and not be pulled tightly against, the threads of the canvas.

Sometimes the yarn becomes twisted as you work. When this happens, simply let the yarn drop freely from the work, and it will naturally untwist itself.

Do not work with a very long length of yarn. Repeated friction against the canvas threads as it is pulled through the mesh will weaken and fray the yarn. About 24 inches is satisfactory.

You will need approximately 1⅓ yards of yarn for each square inch of the design worked in basket weave on No. 10 canvas.

If you go off the diagonal sequence while working the basket weave stitch, don't worry and don't rip the stitches. Simply leave this irregular row as it is and begin again, in the next clear diagonal row to the left, with the diagonal tent stitch. The irregular area can be filled in later with single tent stitches.

If you have to remove stitches, use a sharp, pointed embroidery scissors. Lightly lift each stitch separately and snip the yarn on the right side of the canvas. Be careful not to cut the canvas threads or adjoining stitches.

Stitch a sufficient number of extra rows around the perimeter of the work, so that the design won't be cut off when the finished canvas is framed or seamed. For instance, sew four extra rows if you are making a pillow. To allow for these extra rows of stitches, and for taping the raw edges of the canvas to prevent unraveling, the canvas should be at least 4 inches wider and 4 inches longer than the intended dimensions of the design to be worked on it. There will then be a 2-inch margin of unworked canvas surrounding the area covered by the design.

3. Choosing & Coloring Your Design

There are two classifications of patterns: those whose elements form a picture of a single thing; and those whose elements are simply repeated throughout. The former type of pattern (for example, pattern III-21, page 129) may not easily be cropped without destroying the picture; it may, however, be made larger or smaller by changing the mesh size it is worked on, or by enlarging or reducing the pattern elements (see page 173). Repeat patterns (by far the majority of the patterns) may easily be cropped or extended to conform to specific outside dimensions without changing the mesh size.

An appropriate border may be added to any pattern, either to extend the pattern or to embellish it. Border designs may be obtained from many of the given patterns by extracting just a single row of shapes or elements as shown in Chapter 1, page 12. Many successful border designs consist simply of consecutive rows of stitches in alternate colors, forming a margin of stripes around the design, or rows of a single color forming a solid margin one to two inches wide, which acts as a frame.

As the outside dimensions can be adjusted, the primary consideration in choosing a repeat pattern is its suitability to the finished work. Repeat patterns having large design elements are more suited to larger pieces of work, such as rugs; conversely, those with smaller elements are usually more suitable for smaller objects, such as pillows and handbags.

Designing with Color

There are three basic approaches to the coloring of a design. One is to pick a main, or key, color, and work most or all of the shapes in the design in different shades of this one color. This is called a "monochromatic" color arrangement. Another approach is to use an "adjacent" color scheme, choosing colors that fall next to each other on the color wheel. An arrangement of yellows, greens, and blues would be in this category. The third approach is to pick colors from the complete spectrum, including most or all of the primary and secondary colors, and to balance one hue against another. This is a "polychromatic" color scheme.

A monochromatic arrangement of colors is probably the easiest to handle successfully. It has the advantage of reducing the problem to, basically, a question of light and dark. The key color can be picked to fit the work's intended surroundings. Secondary or tertiary colors can be used as accents. The fact that the design is made up for the most part of a single hue will usually give it a unified appearance.

On the other hand, a polychromatic approach is probably more exciting and absorbing. Interest in the process of sewing is enhanced, since each new color introduced brings a new and unexpected change in the total design, like a story with twists and turns of narrative. The entire range of tonal variations, from very light to very dark, may be used, or the tonal values of the colors may be limited, with only accents of a lighter or darker tone.

An adjacent color scheme falls between these extremes, providing some of the solidity of the monochromatic approach and some of the adventurousness of the polychromatic approach. Such a color scheme has a certain particularity which will not fit in everywhere, but it can be versatile as well. For instance, a pillow of yellows, greens, and blues can fit well into a room which is predominantly either yellow, green or blue, although it will not be harmonious in predominantly red surroundings.

Large or small tracings of the design can be used for color experimentation, using crayons, felt-tipped markers, colored pencils, or watercolors. You may make a small, pencil tracing of the design directly from the line drawing of it in the book and then color it in. In this way, you can quickly and easily make several color sketches and compare them. Your small sketch may look intriguing, but always keep in mind the way your design will look when worked in its actual size. Use these small sketches in conjunction with a full-scale, color sketch traced from the pattern sheet (see page 32). How a pattern is colored will affect the reading of the forms in it, so that often a pattern colored in two different ways will appear to the eye to be two different patterns.

Once you have filled in your colors on either a large or small tracing, you can match the yarn to the sketch. I have found it extremely helpful to take both my colored sketch and the design already marked on the canvas with me to the wool store. In this way I can choose the colors and actually lay them down next to each other in their proper order in the design. Again and again I have had the experience of seeing a color which looks one way in the skein look completely different when placed in the context of the needlepoint design; so this extra caution can be well worth the slight extra trouble it might entail.

Getting Color Ideas

The color photographs in this book show how various people have colored these patterns in their own work. In addition, the black-and-white photographs indicate how different tones may be combined. You may wish to follow these suggestions or to discard them and color the design in your own way.

There are many sources of ideas for coloring your design. Often you may want a piece to fit in a special place—a pillow to be placed on a particular couch, for instance. You might take a color scheme from a drapery or upholstery fabric already used in that room. When designing your work, keep in mind its intended use. A pillow for a brightly colored chair may look best worked in subdued colors, possibly with a bright accent. That way it will not come into conflict with the piece on which it is to be placed. On the other hand, a brightly colored piece of needlework might be just the accent needed to enhance a neutral room.

I like to look for new ideas for coloring my work by studying the fine and decorative art works in museums and in art books. Often, a piece of Oriental ceramics, a miniature painting, or an antique rug will give me an idea for a piece. Books on textile art are especially rich in exciting and unusual themes. It is also interesting to return to the source of the pattern, say a tile wall, and see how it was originally colored by the artists who created it. Most often, though, successful pieces are created purely in relation to the taste of the designer. Use the colors you like best, those which give you the greatest pleasure, and those which best express your feelings about the pattern and the finished piece it will become.

4. Transferring the Design

It is said that there are some talented needlepointers who can work anything on a blank canvas. I have heard stories of those who can simply see a pattern, buy the wool, set to work, and, as if by magic, manage to create a beautiful and complicated piece. However, most people do not fall into this category. Although it is true that the designs in this book are essentially "graphed" patterns and that each could be worked directly from the line drawing, not quite by magic but by determining the number of stitches in a given element and working the same number of stitches on the canvas, most people would feel uncomfortable with this method. Like any counted method, it requires constant attention to the work. A momentary lapse of concentration may result in counting the wrong number of stitches, or in sewing a line in the wrong direction (no matter how familiar the pattern). Mistakes such as these, although never irrevocable in needlepoint (you can simply remove stitches), are annoying nevertheless. Also, once involved in a needlepoint, it is advantageous to be able to work on it anywhere, and at any time—on a train or bus, even while watching television—without having to lug a book along or having to constantly consult cumbersome instruction sheets.

I prefer to have some portion of my design marked on the canvas. Yet, much of the pleasure of working a needlepoint design is in seeing it unfold before your eyes. If the design is already painted in every detail on the canvas before even the first stitch is applied, all the mystery is gone, and with it much of the appeal of the actual work of sewing.

The solution I arrived at was to mark only the outlines of the pattern on the canvas. In that way, I can work my "graphed" patterns without constantly counting stitches, and I can still watch a design unfold as I fill in the outlined areas with each successive color.

My method of putting the design on canvas has two basic steps. The first step is to enlarge the chosen design on a piece of tracing paper placed over pattern sheet I, II, III, or IV. The appropriate pattern sheet depends on which chapter the design comes from. The designs in Chapter 5 are all based on pattern sheet I; those in Chapter 6 are based on pattern sheet II. All the designs in Chapter 7 are based on pattern sheet III and those in Chapter 8 are based on pattern sheet IV. The second step is to use this enlarged tracing as a guide in marking the canvas.

Making the Enlarged Tracing

Enlarging the design not only gives a better picture of what the finished needlepoint will look like, it makes it infinitely easier to mark the canvas. First, pin or tape the pattern sheet for the design you have chosen to a table or other flat surface. (Protect the corners of the pattern sheet by placing permanent pieces of tape there and pinning through or taping over these corners.) Then, pin or tape a sheet of lightweight tracing paper over the pattern sheet. The paper should be translucent enough to allow you to clearly see the pattern sheet beneath it, and it should be large enough to cover the entire pattern sheet. An 18-by-24-inch pad is a commonly available size.

(If you plan to use the enlarged tracing for a color study, you can use a heavier translucent paper, such as vellum or visualizing paper, which takes felt-tipped markers and paints better. Such papers are difficult to see through, however, and it may be necessary to tape the pattern sheet and tracing paper to a light source, such as a light box or window.)

Study the drawn design you wish to enlarge. Each design has a recognizable configuration which is repeated throughout it. In the example shown here (Fig. 43), the configuration of large and small triangles is easily discernible. In some designs, more careful study will be needed in order to perceive and isolate the basic shapes, but this is an important step in copying the design.

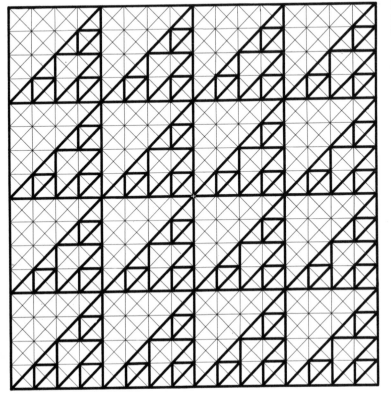

Fig. 43. Each design has a recognizable configuration that will help you copy it. (This is pattern I-11.)

It is helpful to remember that the outlined shapes are based on the given units of the underlying structure represented by the light lines. Look for the largest shape or grouping of shapes covering the greatest number of basic units as the first step. In this design, which is based on a structure of 256 squares, it is apparent that each grouping of large and small triangles covers an area of 16 of these basic-unit squares and that there are 16 such groupings in the entire design. You know, therefore, that the design can be divided into 16 large squares.

As the underlying structure of this design is duplicated by pattern sheet I, once you have the tracing paper pinned or taped over this pattern sheet, you can simply trace the appropriate vertical and horizontal lines on the pattern sheet that will divide the total area of the design into 16 large squares (Fig. 44). Next, you can see that each large triangle covers exactly half the area of one large square. Using the diagonal lines of the pattern sheet as a guide, mark the tracing paper with continuous lines dividing each large square in half (Fig. 45).

Fig. 44. Tape tracing paper over the appropriate pattern sheet and trace the lines that correspond to the unbroken horizontal and vertical lines of the design. (Felt marker is used here for clarity, but it is best to trace with soft pencil first.)

Fig. 45. Trace in the next most evident lines of the design.

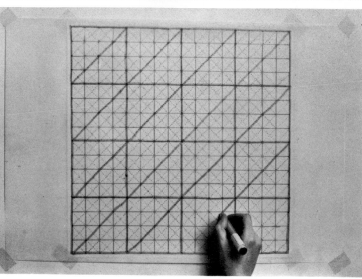

The next largest shape is a medium-sized triangle whose apex meets the base of the large triangle. These triangles are obtained by marking off an area of four basic-unit squares in the right-hand corner of each large square and dividing that area in half with a diagonal line (Fig. 46). Finally, you can mark the smallest elements in this design, the triangles covering one-half of one basic square (Fig. 47).

Fig. 46.   Copy the next largest shapes.

Fig. 47.   Put in the smallest elements of the design.

In this design, many of the lines run unbroken the length or width of the pattern and they provide shortcuts in copying the design. In other designs, there may be different shortcuts which you will discover after looking at the design or after drawing the first two or three shapes. One general rule is to always mark the center of the design area, which is indicated both in the small-scale drawing and on the pattern sheet. This is a good point of reference for copying the design, and the center mark is especially important in those designs where it falls within a design shape, rather than on a dividing line as it does in this design. In designs where the center mark falls within a shape, it will probably be necessary to draw the shape surrounding the center mark onto the tracing paper before proceeding to mark off the rest of the design.

In tracing the design, draw lightly, using a soft pencil. If you wish, you can go over the marked lines with a felt-tipped pen. Use a semi-transparent color (gray, green or light brown, for example) that allows the dotted lines of the pattern sheet to show through but still makes a bold outline.

Although each design is different, all those within a single chapter do share a common underlying structure and root shape. I have also tried to group these designs according to the elements that are stressed, so that each has a logical relationship to the one before or after it. Generally speaking, the designs are also graded within each chapter from simpler ones to successively more complex ones. Don't be intimidated by complex designs, however. Copying one with the aid of the appropriate pattern sheet will give you an understanding of and familiarity with its construction and will make the actual working of it on canvas more pleasurable.

Marking the Canvas

After the design has been traced, it can be transferred to the canvas in the following way. To allow for unworked margins, start with a canvas that is at least 4 inches longer and 4 inches wider than the planned dimensions of your design. Tape the raw edges of the canvas, and, keeping the untaped selvage to the right, mark the top of the canvas. Then fold the canvas in half, and in half again, to find the center. Open the canvas and draw two lines at right angles to each other through the center, dividing the canvas into quarters (Fig. 48). Then mark each of these two lines off with small lines indicating the basic unit of the pattern sheet on which the design is based. These marked center lines are guidelines only and they should be made with a pencil so they can be erased later.

Fig. 48.   Divide the canvas into quarters with two lines at right angles through the center, and mark each of these center lines off with small lines indicating the basic unit of the pattern sheet. (These measurements are detailed separately in the appropriate chapters. Here the lines are marked off into units of 10 threads according to instructions for pattern sheet I.)

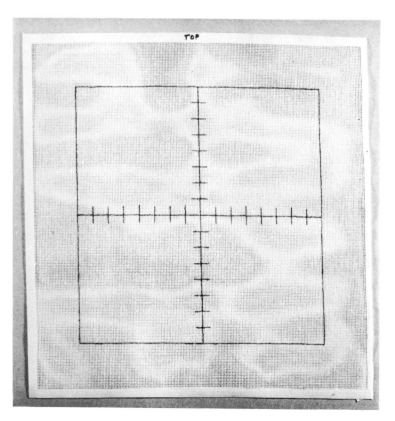

The marked lines can be used as a guide because, although the basic unit on the separate pattern sheets may vary in shape, each can be measured by the number of stitches forming its maximum dimensions horizontally and vertically. The marks along the horizontal center line of the canvas therefore will indicate the unit's maximum horizontal dimension, and the marks along the vertical center line will indicate the unit's maximum vertical dimension. The basic square units in Fig. 48, for instance, measure 10 stitches in each direction.

Starting at the center of the canvas and working outward to the edge of the canvas, you would therefore count off every 10 vertical threads along the drawn horizontal line, and mark each set off as a unit, until you reached the edge of the design area. You would repeat this along the other half of the drawn horizontal line; then, counting off every 10 horizontal threads along the vertical center line, you would mark that off into equal units as well. You would then draw the perimeter of the design area around the marked lines.

Each pattern sheet has its own basic unit and therefore requires a different count in sectioning off the center lines. These counts are given in the separate chapters applying to each pattern sheet. The goal is the same for all the pattern sheets: As these marked center lines on the canvas duplicate the maximum horizontal and vertical measurements of the underlying units on the pattern sheet, they enable you to copy the enlarged tracing, still in position over the pattern sheet, by drawing the design lines from one marked unit on the canvas to another.

In many cases, this can be done in much the same way as the design was traced, by first drawing in the long, unbroken lines of the design, using the guide marks on the canvas to count off the proper number of basic units between horizontal or vertical lines (Fig. 49). In cases where there are no long, unbroken lines running through the design, marking the shapes will be more sequential; starting with the central shape, you can extend the guide marks lightly in pencil to place the first shape on the canvas and build the other lines out from there (Figs. 50 and 51).

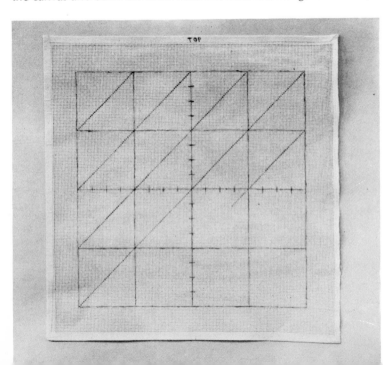

Fig. 49. Copy the design from the tracing onto the canvas, using the marked units as a guide to placing the unbroken horizontal and vertical lines first.

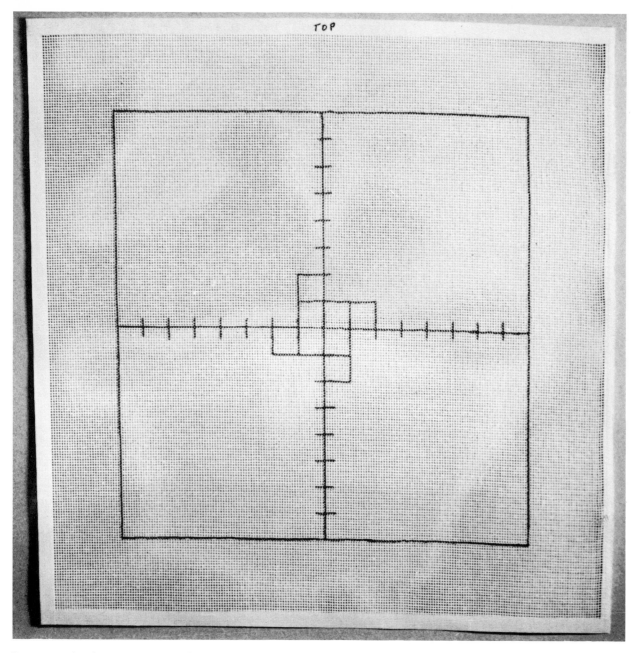

Fig. 50. In this design (Pattern I-1), there are no
unbroken lines, so the central shape is marked on
the canvas first.

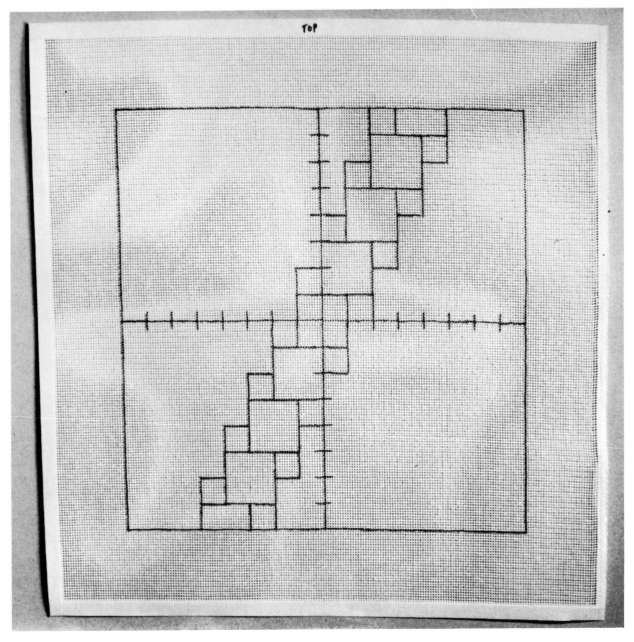

Fig. 51. The other shapes are built out from the central one.

It may sometimes be necessary to count threads within a unit in order to connect certain lines of the design or to draw certain shapes. This should pose no problem because explicit instructions for counting the threads and marking the canvas for such designs are given at the beginning of each chapter in which they appear. In addition, if you are working on No. 10 canvas, you can always place the canvas directly over the enlarged tracing and pattern sheet and see where the line in question should fall.

As the lines of the design will be covered with stitches when you have completed the work, you will not be able to erase them. They must remain on the canvas. Therefore, you must be sure to use a completely waterproof medium for marking any of these designs—so that, when the work is blocked or cleaned, the medium will not run and discolor the surface of the work.

Although many people find using a waterproof marking pen more convenient, I prefer to use acrylic paint applied with a fine-point sable or sabeline brush (No. 3). This medium is 100 percent waterproof, while occasionally a marker that claims to be waterproof is not. Acrylic paint comes in either jars or tubes and in a wide variety of colors. Tubes are easier to handle for our purpose. Use any color which will allow you to see the lines of the design without any trouble, but do not use too dark a color, especially when working with light-colored yarn. (If the design you have chosen is to have outlining stitches, you can match the paint to the intended yarn color.)

Squeeze some paint onto a dish or any other nonabsorbent surface and mix in just enough water to make the medium fluid, so it neither runs nor cakes up. Mark the lines of the design step by step, pausing to redip the brush in water and then in paint as often as necessary to maintain fluidity. Do not fill in design areas with paint, because it tends to make the canvas stiff and difficult to work with. Wash the brush with soap and water immediately after using it; otherwise the paint will dry on the brush and ruin it.

If you wish, you may mark the lines of the design in pencil first, so the lines can be erased in case of a mistake. But you should then go over the pencil marks with paint or a marker. It would not do to leave the markings in pencil; they rub off in handling, and they also dirty the yarn while it is being worked.

If you decide to use a waterproof marking pen, make sure that it is indeed waterproof. Mark a small, test-piece of canvas with the pen; then cover that area with stitches, using a light-colored yarn. Wet this with water. If the stitches are not discolored by the ink from the marking pen, it is suitable for use. If you make a mistake in marking the canvas with a waterproof medium, you can white it out with white acrylic paint or with correction fluid, which is available at stationery or art supply stores.

These are the general rules for transferring the designs to the canvas. Special marking techniques relating to each particular pattern sheet coincide with stitching techniques, both of which are described in the following four chapters.

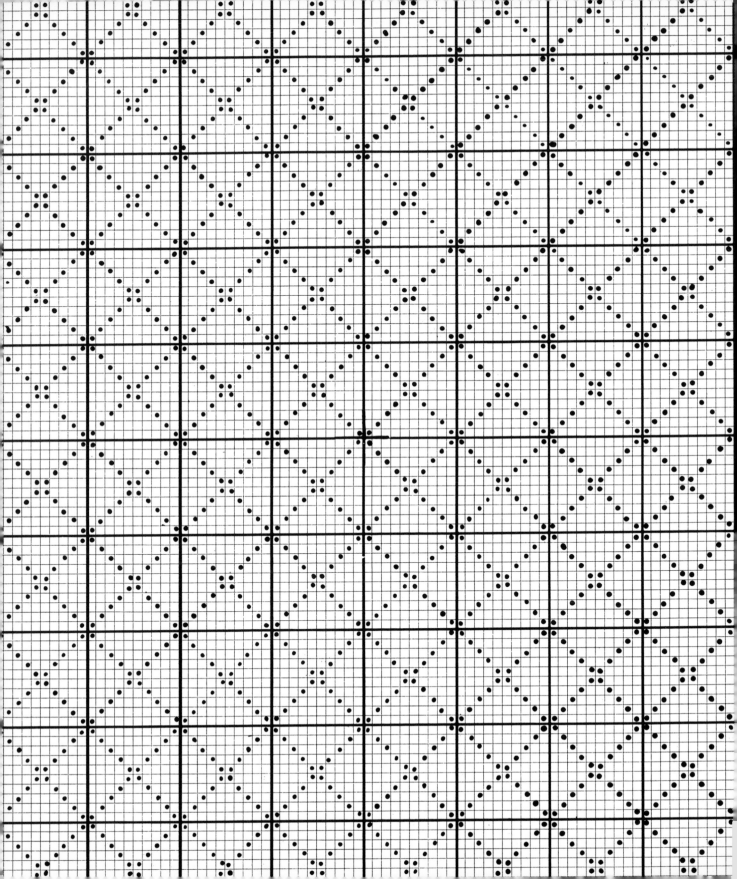

5. Pattern Sheet I: The Even-Numbered Square

This first chapter of patterns emphasizes bold designs that are easy to perceive at a glance. These designs are shaped by areas of tone and color, rather than by line. They depend for their effect upon the symmetry of each shape balancing against its neighbor, of dark against light, negative against positive. A checker pattern is perhaps the simplest form of this kind of design. In a checker pattern, the squares define each other and the pattern becomes apparent only when the squares are filled in. No outline is visible between the squares when the pattern is complete, and none is needed. Like the checker pattern, the designs in this chapter depend entirely upon an interplay of tone and coloring among adjacent shapes.

This means that, when the design is worked on the canvas, the only way that adjacent shapes may be distinguished from each other is by being worked in different colors. In fact, since the shapes must be differentiated by coloration and not by outlines, some of the designs are unrecognizable in purely linear form, and an area of the line drawing for each of these has been filled in to show the design. In order to produce this kind of design in needlepoint, pattern sheet I is constructed so that each basic unit of stitches adjoins the next and is self-contained, not allowing for an extra row of outlining stitches between units. This is explained further in the following paragraphs.

Measuring and Marking

The basic unit of pattern sheet I is a square; the full pattern sheet is 16 units wide and 16 units long, making a total of 256 basic squares. These are designated on the pattern sheet by the heavy lines superimposed on the 10-to-the-inch graph paper. As each box on the graph paper stands for one stitch, you can see that the basic square measures 10 stitches by 10 stitches and that the entire pattern sheet measures 160 stitches horizontally and vertically.

Fig. 52. (Opposite page)   Part of pattern sheet I. Each box of the graph paper stands for one stitch.

Note that the boundary lines between units are drawn between parallel rows of graph boxes. This is because the boxes and therefore the stitches of each unit are counted exclusively. You count off 10 boxes for one unit and begin again with number 1 at the next box (Fig. 53). When you mark these units off on the center lines of the canvas, therefore, you must count the threads in the same way as the boxes: from 1 to 10 and then from 1 to 10 again.

1	2	3	4	5	6	7	8	9	10	1	2	3	4	5	6	7	8	9	10
2	2										2								
3		3									3								
4			4								4								
5				5							5								
6					6						6								
7						7					7								
8							8				8								
9								9			9								
10									10	10									

Fig. 53. Each unit of this pattern sheet measures 10 boxes in each direction. The boxes and therefore the stitches are counted exclusively from 1 to 10 and then from 1 to 10 again. The threads of the canvas are counted in the same way. The numbers in the diagonal boxes here correspond to the dots on the pattern sheet.

The best way to indicate the boundary between two exclusive units on the canvas is to make a line between the last thread of one unit and the first thread of the next unit. To do this, you simply run your pencil, pen or brush in a straight line along the mesh openings between the two parallel threads. In marking horizontal lines, the pencil hits the many small lengths of vertical threads that make up the horizontal mesh row; in marking vertical lines, it hits the small lengths of horizontal threads that make up the vertical mesh row. By marking all horizontal and vertical lines of the design *between* appropriate pairs of *parallel threads* on the canvas, you can see at a glance which adjacent shapes are to be worked in alternate colors (Figs. 54 and 55).

Many of the designs in this chapter also contain diagonal lines. These are indicated on the pattern sheet by the dotted lines running from one corner of a basic unit to the opposite corner. Each diagonal line within a unit also contains 10 stitches counted exclusively. These lines however fall *on* the threads of the canvas, dividing the square unit into two equal triangular ones. In drawing a diagonal line on the canvas, each *intersection* of a vertical and a horizontal thread along the diagonal path is marked off (Fig. 56).

Since the diagonal lines fall *on* the threads, and not between parallel pairs, they provide room for an extra row of stitches between the equal triangles. This extra row is never worked as an outline however; it is always incorporated into the design by being worked in the same color as one of the two triangles. This means that one triangle within a square unit will always be larger than the other one when the design is worked on the canvas.

Fig. 54. Each boundary line between units, represented by the heavy lines on the graph paper, is marked between appropriate pairs of parallel threads on the canvas.

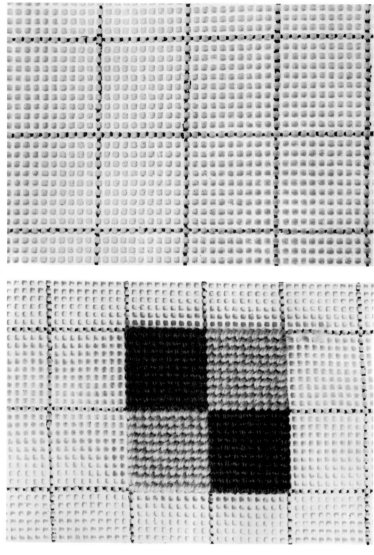

Fig. 55. Adjacent shapes within the marked outlines are filled in with alternate colors.

Fig. 56. Diagonal lines are marked on the intersections of the canvas threads.

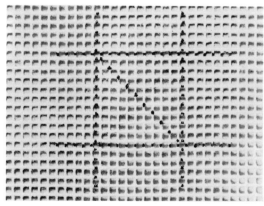

The placement of the larger triangle should be consistent throughout the design. A method of working adjacent triangles so that the large areas are kept constant is described on page 46. In dealing with other shapes that include a diagonal line, the extra row of stitches it provides should again be incorporated in a consistent way. Each design in this chapter that might pose this problem is accompanied by instructions on how to work the diagonal lines.

The diagonal lines actually form eight right-angled triangles—four large ones and four small ones—within each square unit. Although any of these elements may be used in a design, most of the designs in this chapter employ either the entire square or the larger triangular units of the square. When preparing to trace the design, think in terms of the basic square and multiples of it; that is, two or three basic squares form a rectangle, four or eight basic squares form a large square. Similarly, think in terms of which direction the diagonals run and how many squares they dissect. Analyze the shapes outlined by heavy lines on the printed drawing according to how many basic units they cover. As the light lines in the drawing correspond to the heavy lines and dotted diagonals on the pattern sheet, counting off basic units for the enlarged tracing is quite simple.

Fig. 57.   Center guide lines are marked between parallel threads and are marked off in units of 10 threads counted exclusively.

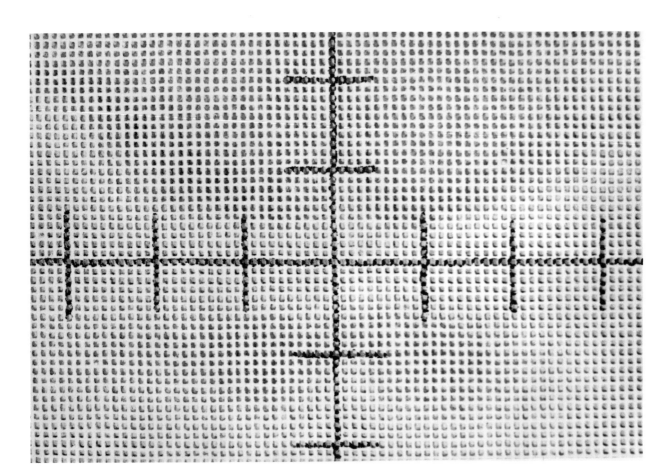

In copying the enlarged tracing onto canvas, begin by taping and folding the canvas as described in Chapter 4. Draw a horizontal and a vertical center line, marking each one *between two parallel threads* of the canvas. Then mark each line off in units of 10 threads counted exclusively (Fig. 57). Begin at the center of the canvas and mark the units out to the edge in each direction until you reach the outside dimensions of the design. The designs in this chapter are all marked on the canvas as described in Chapter 4 and shown in Fig. 58. If a line covers half a unit, count 5 threads exclusively instead of 10. Remember to mark *all* vertical and horizontal lines *between* parallel threads and all diagonal lines *on* the thread intersections.

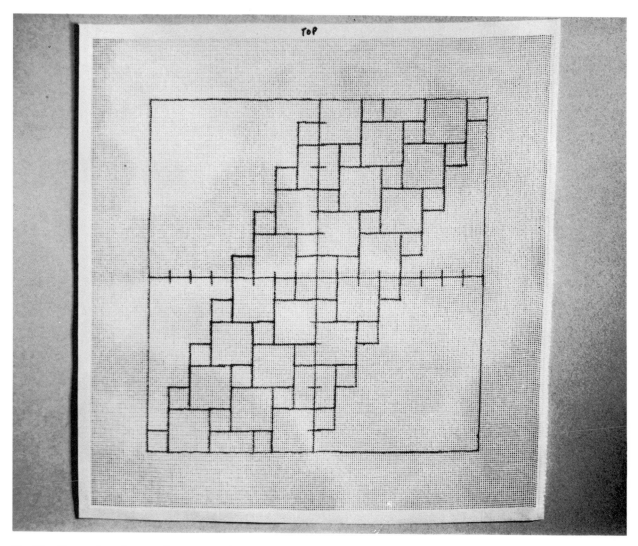

Fig. 58. The sectioned center lines are used to guide the placement of the design lines on the canvas.

Stitching

In working the designs in this chapter, you will be using only the basket weave stitch, to fill in the adjacent shapes. We have already seen how this stitch can be adapted to each shape (Chapter 2). The question may arise, however, as to what sequence is best for filling in the adjacent shapes. This is pertinent when dealing with shapes bounded by diagonal lines because the sequence can help keep the positioning of large and small triangular elements within the design consistent. Taking the pinwheel design on page 52 as an example, we see how the design is marked on the canvas (Fig. 59).

Suppose we begin by making triangle 1 in the uppermost right-hand square the large element and triangle 2 the smaller element in the unit. The easiest way to begin is to use the diagonal tent stitch to cover the diagonal line with light yarn and to fill in triangle 1 with the same yarn, using the diagonal rows of the basket weave. We can then fill in triangle 2 with dark yarn, beginning the basket weave in the upper-right corner as described in Chapter 2, and it will automatically be the smaller element of the unit. As this is a counterchange pattern, we know that triangle 3 will be a dark color, but how do we decide whether it will be the same size as triangle 1 or the size of triangle 2?

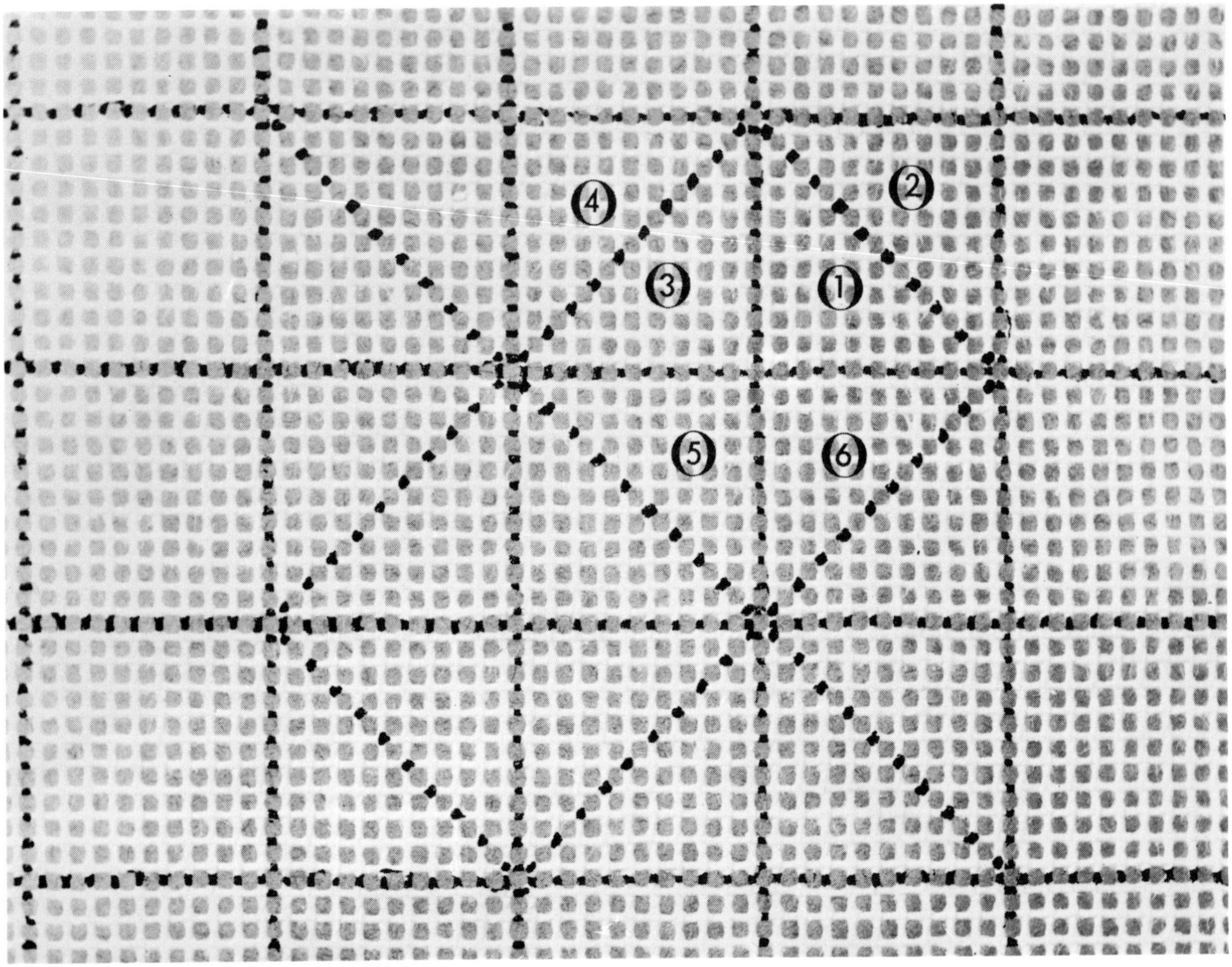

Fig. 59. The pinwheel design of pattern I-5 is marked on the canvas. Note that there are two adjacent thread intersections marked wherever two opposing diagonals meet. The triangular elements 1 through 6 are marked for reference.

Notice the way the threads are marked on the canvas. Wherever two opposing diagonal lines meet, there are two marks side by side forming the apex. This corresponds to the dots on the pattern sheet and it means that the apex is always formed by two stitches, not by just one. Triangle 3 therefore must be worked so that it incorporates the diagonal line marked on the canvas; it will thus be the same size as triangle 1. The basket weave begun as shown in Fig. 40, page 25, is the most appropriate for this triangle. When triangle 3 is finished, triangle 4 may be filled in by turning the work upside down and using the same sequence of stitches used for triangle 3, and it will automatically be the same size as triangle 2.

If you look again at the lines drawn on the canvas, you will see that now triangles 5 and 6 must also be worked so that they incorporate their diagonal lines and thus form a two-stitch apex wherever their diagonals meet opposing ones.

Fig. 60 shows how the four triangles will look after they have been completed. Remember that there must be two stitches at the apex and that this rule applies whenever there are opposing diagonals that meet, whether the colors of the adjacent shapes are the same or are different and whether the shape is a triangle, diamond, or parallelogram. This is why, once it was established that triangle 1 covered its diagonal line, triangles 3, 5, and 6 had to cover their diagonal lines.

Fig. 60. Triangles 1, 2, 3, and 4 are worked in a logical order to keep the positioning of the large and small triangular elements consistent. Triangles 1 and 3 are the large ones. Note that there are two stitches at each apex.

Pattern I-1

This is a simple geometric design composed of small and large squares. The small squares are one-quarter the size of the large squares. The large squares are arranged in a steplike configuration, with the small squares filling the spaces between.

Fig. 61. A portion of pattern I-1 made into a small pillow by Doris Gluck. The larger squares are alternately olive green and turquoise blue; a salmon red is used as a bright accent color for all the small squares. The face of the pillow measures 11 by 11 inches, worked on No. 10 mesh.

Pattern I-2

This design, which appears in Russian ornament, is composed of two shapes: a square and a rectangle. One possibility for coloring is to make each of the four rectangles surrounding a square a different color, but always in the same order. In this way, the rectangles will appear to be strips which weave over and under each other. All squares could then be made one color, or various colors, whichever is preferred. An ambitious designer might want to create a counter-pattern within the squares, using smaller squares or using triangles.

This pattern is especially easy to construct because it is divided by unbroken lines running the length and width of the pattern into large squares, each measuring 4 basic units by 4 basic units.

I-2

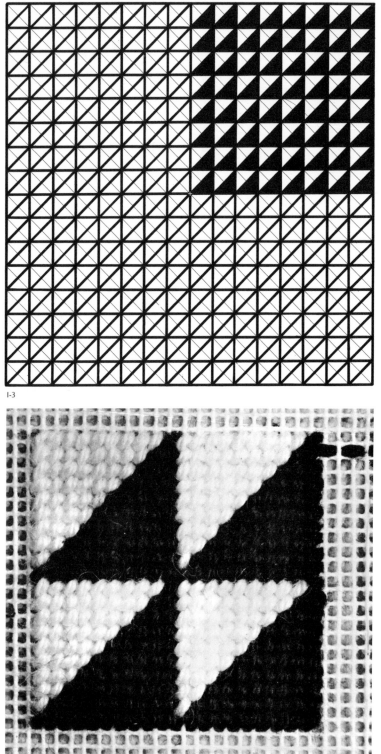

I-3

Pattern I-3

This pattern and the following seven are what is called "counterchange patterns," a type of design that grew out of the art of mosaic. (Many of the counterchange patterns here were in fact derived from the mosaic floor of the Baptistry in Florence, Italy.) Using identically shaped tiles, a dark tile is mirrored by a light one. This interplay of reverses, this "counterchange," creates the rhythm of the design.

These patterns become readable as designs only when the shapes are filled in. Otherwise they look like mere networks of crossing lines. Therefore, I have filled in the shapes in one-quarter of the pattern area to show how the design should read; the rest of the pattern is in line form to show the structure of the design.

Any of these counterchange patterns may be used alone, in combination with each other, or with other patterns from this chapter. They may be worked in two colors or in as many colors as you wish, as long as you retain the proper dark-and-light relationship.

Pattern I-3 is of light and dark triangles formed by diagonal lines which go in a single direction. Each unit is exactly the same as all the other units in the pattern. When worked in needlepoint, this pattern has an even and regular appearance, because the diagonal lines of the pattern slant in the same direction as the tent stitches, from upper right to lower left (Fig. 62).

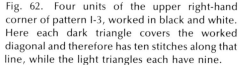

Fig. 62. Four units of the upper right-hand corner of pattern I-3, worked in black and white. Here each dark triangle covers the worked diagonal and therefore has ten stitches along that line, while the light triangles each have nine.

50

Pattern I-4

These light and dark triangles are based on diagonal lines that go in opposing directions. Each unit is the reverse image of the unit horizontally adjacent to it. When this pattern is worked in needlepoint (Fig. 63), some of the diagonals are even-looking lines, while others have a serrated appearance. This is due to the very nature of the tent stitch, which is always worked in the same direction, no matter what kind of line it is describing.

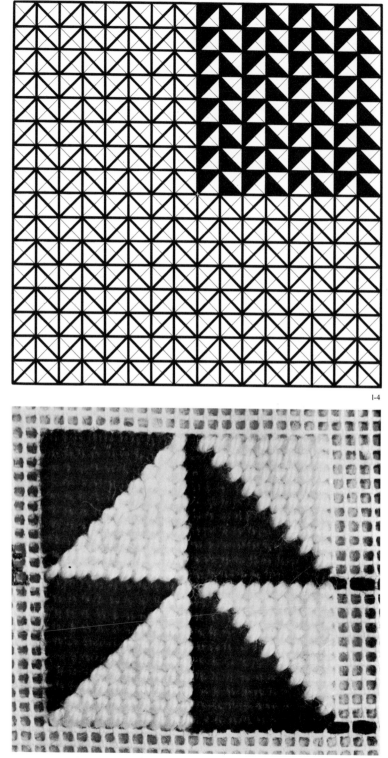

I-4

Fig. 63. Four units of the upper right-hand corner of pattern I-4, worked in black and white. In this example, the bottom triangle of each square covers the marked diagonal, and each top triangle is smaller by one stitch along its diagonal, regardless of the triangle's color.

I-5

Pattern I-5

These light and dark triangles are also formed with opposing diagonals. Here, each unit is the reverse image of the unit adjacent to it both horizontally and vertically. When it is worked in patchwork the pattern is called a "pinwheel."

This pattern forms the center design in the sampler shown in Fig. 64, which can serve as an excellent learning piece to gain experience in working the basket weave stitch. All starting sequences described in Chapter 2 are included. (The border squares are worked as in Fig. 38; the center triangles are worked as in Figs. 39 and 40.) Having completed this piece you will have little trouble working the basket weave stitch for any pattern in the book.

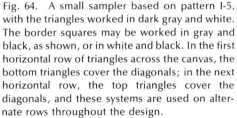

Fig. 64. A small sampler based on pattern I-5, with the triangles worked in dark gray and white. The border squares may be worked in gray and black, as shown, or in white and black. In the first horizontal row of triangles across the canvas, the bottom triangles cover the diagonals; in the next horizontal row, the top triangles cover the diagonals, and these systems are used on alternate rows throughout the design.

Pattern I-6

A zigzag pattern of alternating dark and light parallelograms. To work this pattern in needlepoint so that each shape is equal in size, begin with the first dark parallelogram in the upper right-hand corner. Start at the top diagonal with the diagonal tent stitch and work the basket weave down to, but do not cover with stitches, the parallel diagonal line below. Change to light-colored yarn and work that line; then work the rest of the shape down to the next marked diagonal without covering it. Change to dark yarn, and work down to the third diagonal without covering it. Follow this principle to fill in all the shapes. When working the adjacent vertical row, remember that the opposing diagonals must have two stitches at their apex, in this case one dark and one light stitch. (The parallelograms based on the upper-right-to-lower-left diagonal may be worked as in Fig. 40, Chapter 2.)

I-6

Fig. 65. Nine units of the upper right-hand corner of pattern I-6, worked in black and white. Each parallelogram measures ten stitches vertically and diagonally.

I-7

Pattern I-7

Each of the light and dark triangles has a base measuring two units. In this pattern, it is best to work the horizontal rows of triangles across the canvas, rather than to work the shapes in vertical rows. Starting in the upper right-hand corner, the dark triangles will cover the drawn diagonal lines. In the next horizontal row, the light triangles cover the drawn diagonals. The third row is worked in the same way as the first; the fourth, the same as the second, and so on.

Fig. 66. Twelve units of the upper-right hand corner of pattern I-7, worked in black and white.

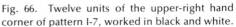

54

Pattern I-8

This pattern combines light and dark triangles and parallelograms (see needlepoint belt in color on page 159). It is best worked by starting at the upper right side with the first large, white triangle. (Begin the triangle with the diagonal tent stitch.) Work the entire triangle to cover the lower marked diagonal line as well as the top. All light and dark triangles horizontally along this row (Row 1 on the line drawing) will cover *both* marked diagonals. (Begin the dark triangles as in Fig. 40.) Triangles horizontally along Row 2 on the line drawing will not cover either marked diagonal. All odd-numbered rows will be the same as Row 1, where the stitches of the triangles *do* cover the marked diagonals; all even-numbered rows will be the same as Row 2, where the stitches of the triangles *do not* cover the marked diagonal lines. Work all the triangles first. The remaining shapes (the parallelograms) can then be filled in alternately with dark and light-colored yarn.

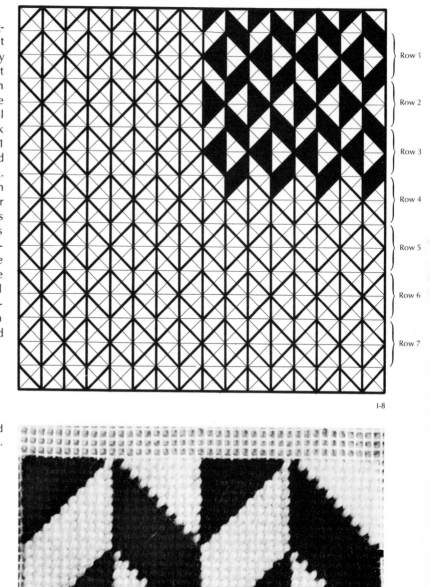

Row 1
Row 2
Row 3
Row 4
Row 5
Row 6
Row 7

I-8

Fig. 67. Sixteen units of the upper right-hand corner of pattern I-8, worked in black and white.

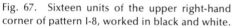

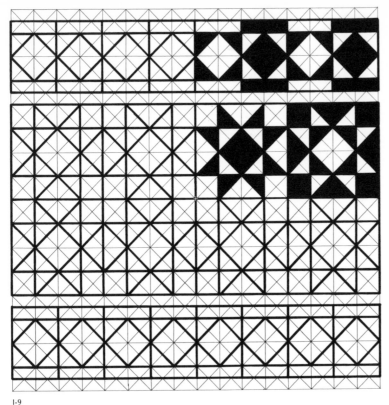

I-9

Pattern I-9

This line drawing combines two counter-change patterns. Both of these designs appear often in Renaissance painting as decorative insets and borders, and in architecture as inlaid floor designs and wall panels. The design can be used in its entirety, or you can use either motif alone, as either a band or an overall design. The center motif, enlarged, is used in the patchwork pattern on page 186.

Fig. 68. Border design. The center diamonds have nine stitches along each diagonal; the surrounding triangles have ten.

Fig. 69. A variation of the eight-pointed star motif, worked in three tones. All light triangles have ten stitches along the diagonal; so do the small black triangles. The large black triangles have nine stitches along each diagonal, as do the medium-toned triangles and diamond.

Pattern I-10

This handsome geometric pattern creates an optical illusion of three dimensions when worked in tones ranging from light to dark (Fig. 70). The center motif alone can be repeated to create an entirely new and different design (Fig. 71).

Fig. 70. A portion of pattern I-10 worked in black, white, ecru, and tones of gray to show the importance of tonal arrangement in the creation of this pattern. The triangles and trapezoids could be tones of a single color; the bordering rectangles could be an accenting or complementary color. Each triangle and trapezoid with a horizontal base covers the marked diagonal and has ten stitches along that line; each shape with a vertical base has nine stitches along its diagonal.

I-10

Fig. 71. The center motif is used alone and repeated in four adjacent squares. The darkest and lightest triangles (those having a horizontal base) cover the marked diagonals.

57

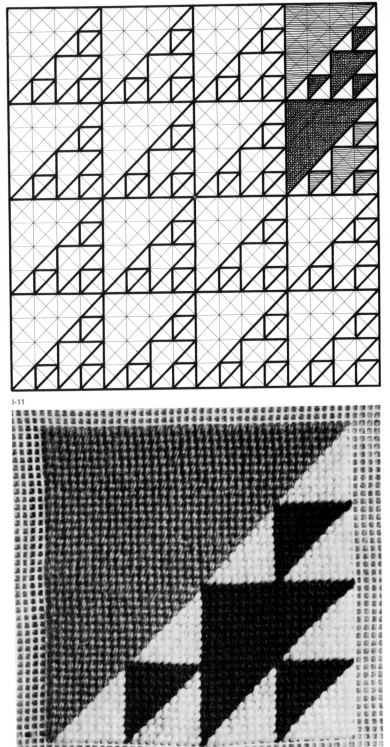

I-11

Pattern I-11

This simple but interesting pattern of triangles arranged within squares is derived from Byzantine gold enameling, an art praised by poet William Butler Yeats: *But such a form as Grecian goldsmiths make/Of hammered gold and gold enameling/To keep a drowsy Emperor awake;/Or set upon a golden bough to sing/To lords and ladies of Byzantium/Of what is past, or passing, or to come.*

The charm of this pattern is greatly increased if the triangles are worked with alternate color arrangements. One possibility is illustrated in the line drawing. Color all triangles in the first horizontal row of shapes across the design as shown in the top-right square. Color all triangles in the next horizontal row of shapes as shown in the square below that. Color the next two horizontal rows alternately, like the first two.

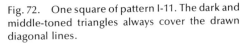

Fig. 72. One square of pattern I-11. The dark and middle-toned triangles always cover the drawn diagonal lines.

Pattern I-12

In this pattern a heightened three-dimensional effect is created through the use of dark, light, and middle tones. In the case of the design used in the needlepoint pillow (Fig. 73), light seems to be shading the top and right side of each "building-like" configuration. This pattern is derived from Russian ornament.

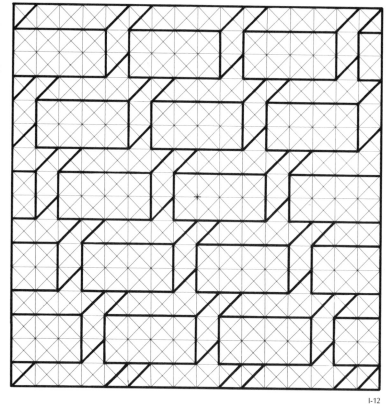

I-12

Fig. 73. This striking needlepoint pillow, by Dorothy Litoff, is worked in three shades of brown, on No. 12 mesh. The darkest tone will cover the marked diagonal lines.

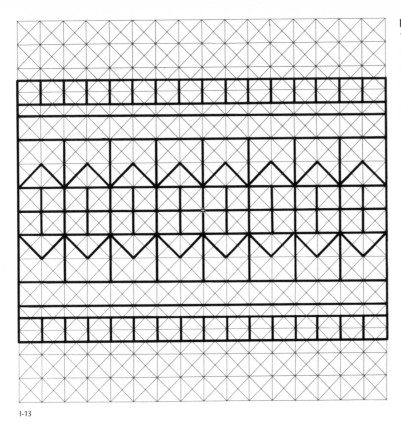

I-13

Pattern I-13

This pattern is a variation of an Egyptian border design found on mummy cases now in the British Museum and the Louvre. However, the "M" doesn't stand for "mummy," or anything else, as far as I know. The smaller bands within the pattern are each a half-unit high, or five stitches.

Each diagonal line in the "M" is made up of three rows of stitches: one along the drawn diagonal and one above and below it. Each vertical line should have two rows of stitches—one on either side of the drawn dividing line. The "M"'s should be worked first.

Fig. 74. Needlepoint pillow designed by Winifred Bendiner and worked by Muriel Kahn. Worked on No. 10 mesh with tapestry yarn in red, yellow, dark green, and two shades of blue. (See color page 158.)

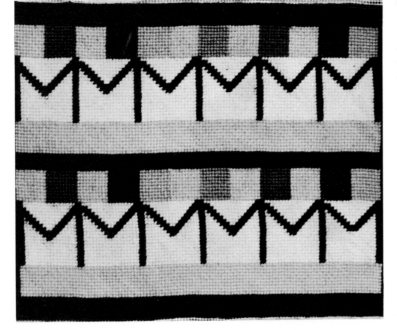

Fig. 75. A variation of pattern I-13, by Netty Cohen. The bands are separated and face the same direction. The vertical stems of each "M" are two rows wide, and the diagonals three rows wide. (See color page 158.)

Pattern I-14

This pattern illustrates perhaps best of all the relation of these designs to basket weaving, since it literally originated as a plaited straw pattern from the South Sea Islands. Early European voyagers to the South Seas wrote of their astonishment in finding designs "in such an endless variety of figures that one might suppose [the islanders] borrowed their patterns from a mercer's shop in which the most elegant productions of China and Europe [were] collected."

The line drawing of this pattern is 14 by 11½ units, because that cropping of the repeat is the most satisfactory.

To maintain the symmetry of the shapes, start each shape at point A in the drawing and cover the four diagonals at the top of the shape; work down to the next four diagonals in the shape below without covering them. Change to the alternate color to cover those diagonals and work down to the next four diagonals without covering them.

Fig. 76. Begin each shape with the diagonal at the far right. Cover all the diagonals at the top of the shape. The diagonals at the bottom of the shape belong to the next unit and are covered by the alternate color.

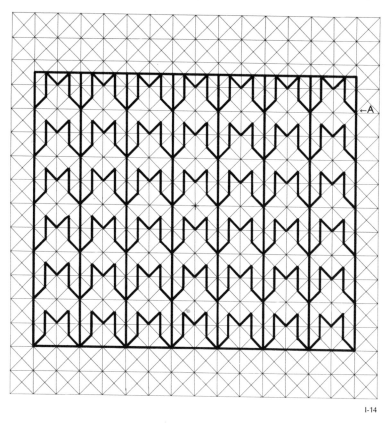

←A

I-14

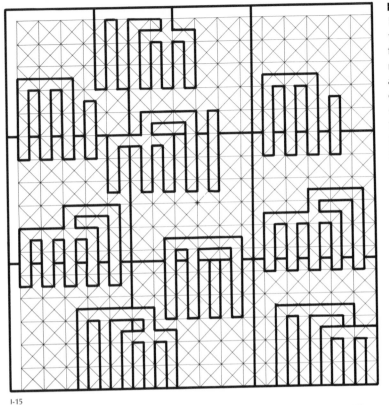

I-15

Pattern I-15

I transposed this design from one found on the skirt-like trousers *(hangire)* worn by performers in a Japanese No play. In the original, the characters were appliquéd in gold and stood for chapters of the classic "Tales of Gengi," though they were applied to the costumes more as a decorative device than to convey literal meaning. The coloring of the original is maintained in the needlepoint (see color page 158 as well as Fig. 77).

Fig. 77. Needlepoint pillow designed by Susan Schoenfeld and worked on No. 12 mesh by Nancy Finklestein. The characters are worked in rayon thread. An inch-wide white border frames the design.

Pattern I-16

This pattern achieves its full eye-catching and hypnotic quality only when colored with the highest possible contrast. When so colored, the shapes seem to converge toward, then disperse from, the center like a neon sign (see color page 158 as well as Fig. 78).

To insure symmetry, this design is best worked in two halves, first working the lower half, and then turning the work upside down and working the other half in exactly the same way. To work the lower half, start at the center and fill in the dark chevron shape. Cover the upper diagonal lines of this shape, but do not cover the lower ones. Next, fill in the light-colored parallelograms to either side, covering the upper diagonal lines but not the lower ones. Continue filling in the remaining chevrons and parallelograms in the lower half of the design following the same principle.

Where the diagonals are at the sides of the parallelogram, the marked line on the left side of the shape will be covered for each shape in the left-hand section of the canvas; and the marked line at the right side of the shape will be covered for each shape in the right-hand section. Omit the horizontal row of chevrons (these will be filled in last). Turn the work and fill in the unworked half in exactly the same way. Then complete the piece by filling in the center, horizontal chevron shapes.

I-16 (Note: The center of this pattern is not in the middle of the pattern sheet. To center it on the canvas after it has been traced, see page 71.)

Fig. 78. Needlepoint designed by Howard Kalish; worked by Nancy and Howard Kalish, on No. 10 mesh with tapestry yarn.

6. Pattern Sheet II: The Odd-Numbered Square

The designs in this chapter, like those in the preceding one, are based on the square and its diagonals. But here the designs derive their beauty from their linear structures and do not rely solely on tonal differentiation between shapes. These designs are clearly recognizable whether they are seen with the shapes filled in or in outline form alone.

Many of these designs originated as lattice work; they were used to create a decorative, fence-like structure of wooden or metal strips for windows, doors, railings, and gates. Since they were executed with strips of material, the designs were essentially linear and their effect came from the many fascinating and intricate patterns the lines themselves could be made to form.

They are used here as colored designs, but the outlines remain as the prime structural elements. In order to allow for these outlines, pattern sheet II is constructed on the basis of *inclusively* counted units.

Fig. 79. (Opposite page)   Part of pattern sheet II.

Measuring, Marking, and Stitching

Although there are still 256 basic squares cut by their diagonals, each unit of this pattern sheet measures 11 graph boxes horizontally, vertically, and diagonally, and each is marked by dotted lines connecting the **X**'s at each of its four corners. The graph boxes, and therefore the threads and stitches, of each unit are counted from 1 to 11, and the last box or stitch counted becomes the first box or stitch for the next unit (Fig. 80). As a result, the basic units of pattern sheet II are not self-contained; each unit overlaps the next unit by one horizontal and one vertical row of boxes on the pattern sheet and by one horizontal and one vertical row of stitches on the canvas. As you will see, this inclusive method of counting produces an extra row of stitches between two equal and adjacent shapes and makes it possible to outline the shapes.

When the horizontal and vertical lines of the designs are transferred to the canvas, they are marked *on* the horizontal and vertical threads of the canvas (Fig. 81). They then become sewn boundaries as shown in Fig. 82. The areas outlined in this way are identical to each other in size and shape because the boundary is sewn on the extra thread of the canvas corresponding to the row of overlapping boxes on the pattern sheet. The diagonal lines of the designs are marked, as before, on the intersections of the threads, where they too become sewn boundaries. Note that wherever opposing diagonals meet on this pattern sheet there is only one stitch.

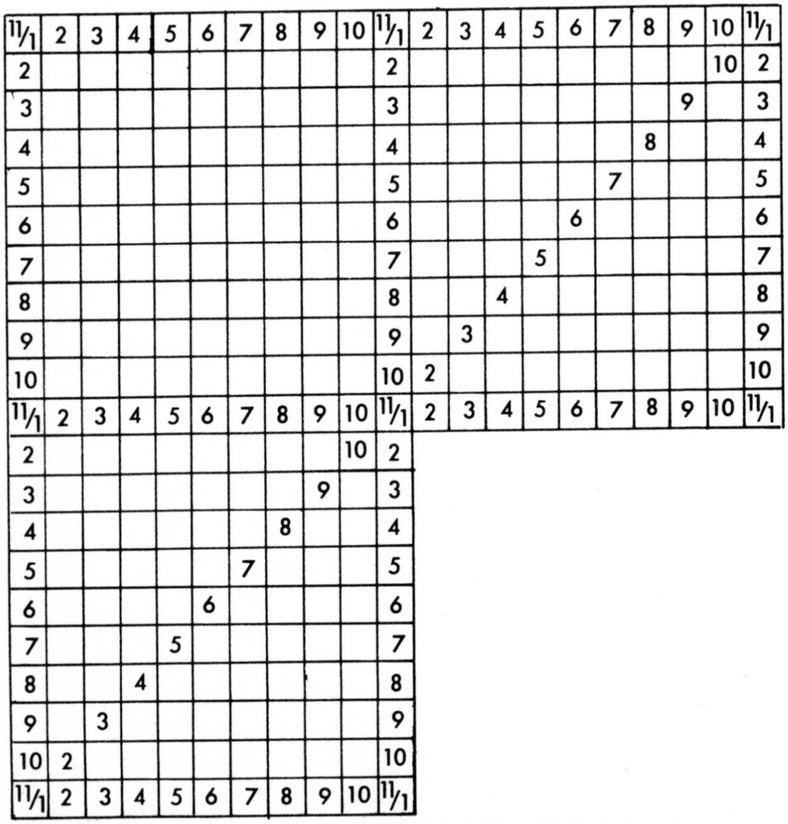

Fig. 80. Each unit of this pattern sheet measures 11 boxes in each direction. The boxes and therefore the threads and stitches are counted inclusively; the last box counted for one unit becomes the first box for the next unit. The single numbers here correspond to the dots on the pattern sheet; the double numbers correspond to the **X**'s.

The linear aspects of the design may be emphasized by working the boundaries in one color and filling in the shapes with a contrasting color. Alternately, an outline may be obscured by making it the same color as the shape it defines. However, because the outlines are indispensable as structural elements in these designs, they are always worked on the canvas first, with the appropriate outlining stitches described in Chapter 2, and the remaining areas are filled in later with the basket weave stitch.

Tracing a design from this chapter is essentially no different from the procedure used with pattern sheet I. You need only remember that the light lines in the drawing correspond to the dotted lines of this pattern sheet. It is then a simple matter to count the number of units a line covers on the drawing and duplicate the line on the tracing paper placed over the pattern sheet.

Fig. 81. Each horizontal and vertical line is marked on the horizontal or vertical threads of the canvas.

Fig. 82. The outlines marked on the canvas in this way then become sewn boundaries between adjacent shapes.

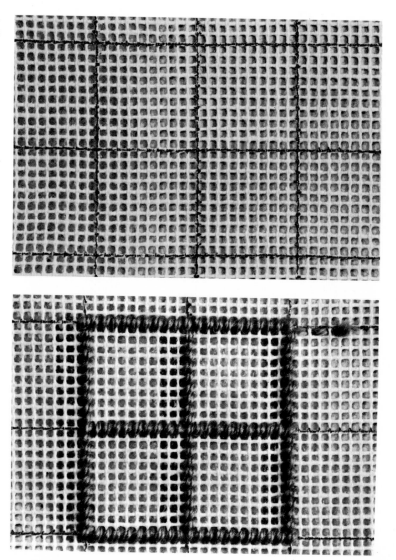

In marking the canvas, begin with the center lines marked off into units of 11 threads horizontally and vertically (Fig. 83). The difference here is that you must count the threads, like the boxes, *inclusively*. One unit measures 11 threads, but two units measure 21 threads, not 22. If you wish to determine the length of a line covering more than one unit of the pattern sheet, you can simply multiply the number of units it covers by 10 and add 1. Thus if a line covers 1½ units on the pattern sheet, it will measure 16 stitches (10 × 1½ + 1) on the canvas. If it covers ½ unit, it will measure 6 stitches (10 × ½ + 1). The entire pattern sheet measures 161 stitches in each direction.

You must also draw *all* the horizontal and vertical lines of the design *on* the corresponding threads of the canvas. This is true for the center lines as well as for the design lines (Fig. 84).

Many of the designs in this chapter contain lines that can be measured by single units and half units. To mark the design shown here, for instance, you need only count 6 thread intersections and 11 horizontal threads to place all of the lines (Fig. 85).

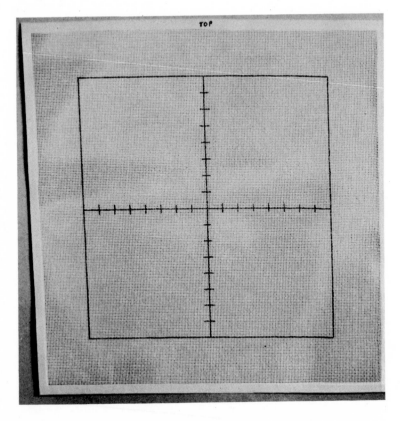

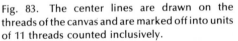

Fig. 83. The center lines are drawn on the threads of the canvas and are marked off into units of 11 threads counted inclusively.

Fig. 84. Use the sectioned guide lines to place the design on the canvas, marking horizontal and vertical lines on the threads and diagonal lines on the thread intersections.

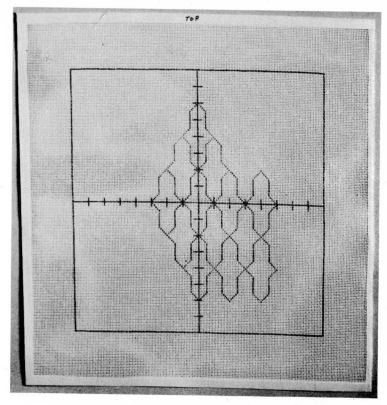

Fig. 85. It is often possible to mark the design by merely counting either 6 or 11 threads. Note that wherever the lines meet there is an inclusively counted thread.

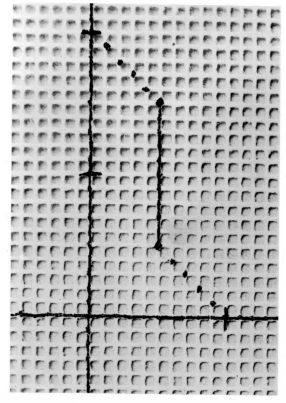

One final note: For some of the designs in this chapter, it may be necessary to draw the center rules off-center on the canvas. These are designs that contain an odd number of units, either horizontally or vertically, or in both directions (such as 15 units by 15 units instead of 16 by 16), so that the center of the design (marked by a circle) no longer coincides with the center of the pattern sheet (Fig. 86). As a result, you can no longer place the guide lines in the center of the canvas if you wish to have equal margins around the design.

Fig. 86. A design, such as II-24, containing an odd number of units has its center marked by a circle in the drawing. As this center does not coincide with the center of the pattern sheet (also marked on the drawing), the design must be drawn off-center on the canvas.

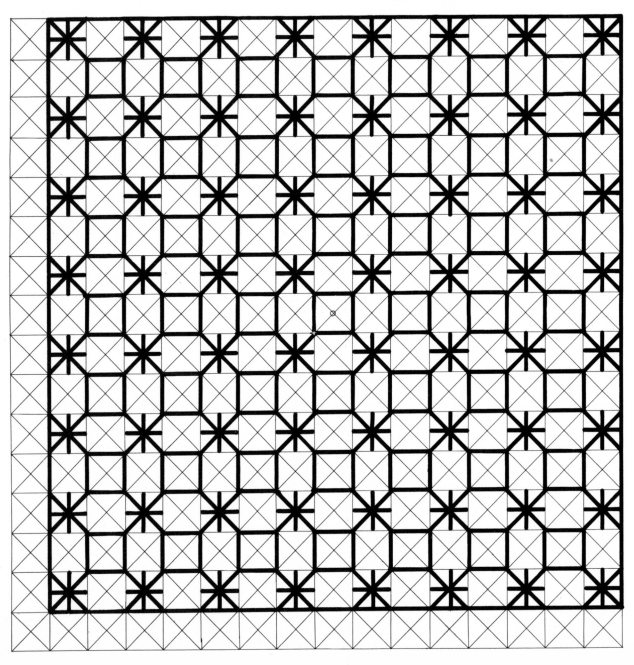

Instead you must place the circle of the design in the center of the canvas and draw the center guide lines off-center on the canvas. Mark both the center of the design and the center of the pattern sheet on the enlarged tracing and measure the distance between the two according to the number of graph boxes on the pattern sheet beneath the tracing. For instance, the center mark of the pattern sheet is six boxes below the center of this design.

Obtain the actual center of the canvas in the usual way, by folding the canvas into quarters. This becomes the center of the design. Since the center of the pattern sheet is six boxes *below* the center of the design, you must count six thread intersections down from the actual center of the canvas, along the same diagonal path. The last intersection counted becomes the center point for your horizontal and vertical guide lines, which can now be marked on the canvas (Fig. 87).

Fig. 87. The actual center of the canvas becomes the center of the design, and the guide lines are drawn through a new center point on the canvas. This point is the same distance from the actual center of the canvas as the center of the design is from the center of the pattern sheet shown on the drawing.

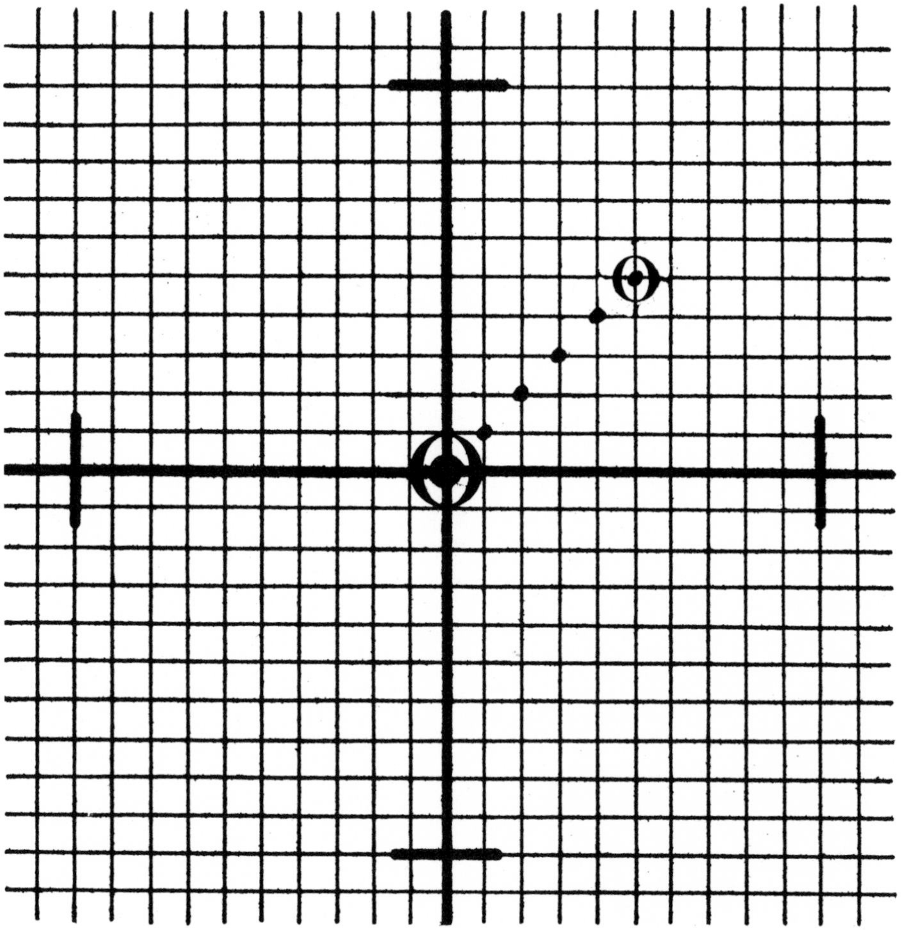

actual center of canvas

new center point for horizontal and vertical rules

71

II-1

Pattern II-1

A network of diamond shapes (which are actually squares on end) is created by using just the diagonal lines of the pattern sheet. A simple configuration such as this can become a beautiful design by filling in the design with colors and tones that stress the shapes rather than the outlines. Many exquisite ceramic-tile walls have been created in just this way, by placing many single-shaped tiles of different colors in a pleasing and harmonious arrangement. The needlepoint shown in Fig. 88 (see also the color picture on page 162) is adapted from a mosaic tile-pattern in the Alhambra, a palace built in Granada, Spain, by the Moors, primarily during the thirteenth and fourteenth centuries.

The area of diamonds in Fig. 88, like that of the drawn design, measures the full 16 units vertically and 15 units horizontally. The diamonds are bordered by rectangular shapes, each measuring 3 units by 1 unit. Each of the pointed forms in the outside border has a broad base of 3 units; these shapes are made by starting at the base and stitching the following outlining sequences: (describing the forms at the top and bottom of the border) a 6-stitch diagonal, an 11-stitch vertical, a 6-stitch horizontal, an 11-stitch vertical, and a 6-stitch diagonal; (describing the forms at the sides of the border) a 6-stitch diagonal, an 11-stitch horizontal, a 6-stitch vertical, an 11-stitch horizontal, and a 6-stitch diagonal. The entire design is first outlined with white yarn, and then filled in with green and orange, shades of blue, and white.

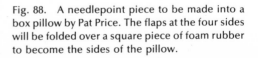

Fig. 88. A needlepoint piece to be made into a box pillow by Pat Price. The flaps at the four sides will be folded over a square piece of foam rubber to become the sides of the pillow.

Pattern II-2

Fig. 89 illustrates how a simple, linear pattern can be worked to emphasize the lines themselves by sewing an additional row of stitches to either side of each line. This pattern is well-suited to such treatment, since the combination of diagonal and vertical lines itself produces a varied and decorative effect. In the Indian miniature painting from which this pattern was taken, the center line describing the shape was black; the two lines flanking it were white, and all the shapes were filled in with a light pink. In coloring your own work though, there is no reason to keep all the shapes a single color, as long as you do not let a too-elaborate coloring pattern confuse the basic design.

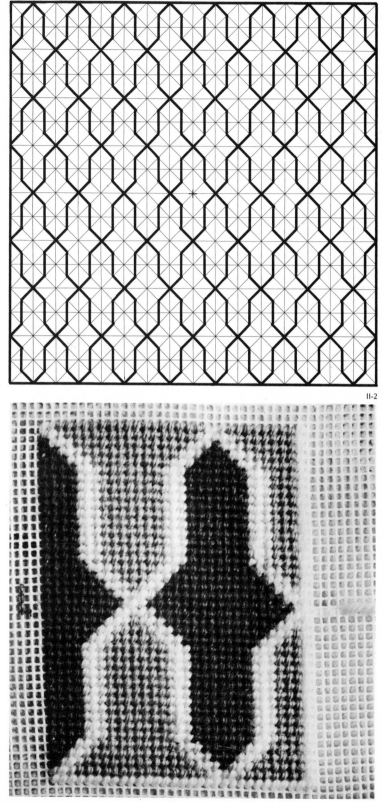

II-2

Fig. 89. The rhythmic linear quality of pattern II-2 is emphasized by working an extra row of stitches to either side of the outline. This technique works well with many of the patterns in this chapter. Here the stitched outline is white and the row to each side of it is ecru; the shapes are filled in with two tones of gray.

II-3 (Off-center pattern: see pages 70-71)

Pattern II-3

This geometric pattern, though still made up of only one shape, is more complex than the previous patterns. It can be worked with subdued or stressed outlines and it can be colored to either retain the feeling of an overall design or to emphasize separate aspects of it. In Fig. 90, the outlined shapes are colored to accent the center and the corners of the design.

Fig. 90. This needlepoint design by Grace Kaplan is worked in yellow and three shades of green, with the darkest green used for outlining.

Pattern II-4

This design is from a fifteenth-century decoration in a house in Cairo, Egypt. I must admit it is one of my favorites. I am fascinated by the way the leaflike shapes seem to be facing in four directions at once. (For this reason, this kind of pattern is called a "quartered counterchange.") The same pattern is shown enlarged and used for appliqué on page 181).

II-4 (Off-center pattern: see pages 70-71)

Fig. 91. Needlepoint pillow by Phyllis Florman. The design is outlined with light purple yarn; the 16 shapes that appear to form a medium-light background in the center are also filled in with that color. This coloration makes the outline invisible except where the darkest shapes meet the lightest ones at the outside edges of the design. These light shapes are yellow; the dark shapes are deep purple, the center shape is white, and the 9 medium-toned shapes are green.

II-5

Pattern II-5

This Japanese pattern is actually a continuous, meandering line constructed upon only the diagonal lines of the pattern sheet. This kind of pattern is known as a fret pattern. The Greeks first used continuous-line or fret patterns as border designs on painted urns. Later examples are found in Roman and in medieval Christian art. Independently, the Japanese and Chinese each developed the art of fret ornament to a high degree of refinement, as shown by this skillful example.

Fig. 92. The primary outline is expanded with additional rows. The primary outline is dark. It is flanked on either side by a medium-dark row and then another dark row. The remaining areas are filled in with light-colored yarn. The overall effect is of an equal dark-and-light pattern with each area measuring 5 stitches wide. (The 11-stitch measurement of each unit is formed by 5 light stitches bounded on either side by a dark, medium, and dark stitch.) A practical reason for using the medium-dark color is to help you keep track of the primary outline.

Fig. 93.   An eyeglass case, worked in petit point, of blue and green silk and gold thread. (From Chinese textile collection, eighteenth to nineteenth century, at the Metropolitan Museum of Art, Bequest of William Christian Paul, 1930.) Pattern II-5 appears as a background design, with free-form leaf shapes superimposed over it.

II-6

Pattern II-6

This pattern, named "fish-net," is also Japanese. The needlepoint shown in Fig. 94 illustrates a design idea that can be used with many of the patterns given here, namely, treating each outlined shape autonomously and filling each one in with stitches worked as striped or other small-scale designs.

Fig. 94.   Freely interpreted needlepoint by Yetta Kalish. Some areas have been filled in with stripes.

Pattern II-7

This lattice pattern is formed by large diamonds which overlap. As a result of this overlapping, the lines also form medium-sized diamonds, small diamonds, and cross-shapes. How the design appears when it is worked is governed in large part by how it is colored; Fig. 95 is one example from many possibilities.

II-7

Fig. 95.   A detail of pattern II-7, worked in dark gray, black and white. This is a good example of how one may hide the outline in coloring a design. The outlining color (dark gray) is the same as the larger diamonds; therefore it is hidden where it borders those shapes, and, because of the closeness of tone, it virtually disappears where it borders the smaller, black diamonds.

II-8a

II-8b

Pattern II-8

This Chinese lattice pattern is given in two forms, *a* and *b*, the shapes of the latter one being half the size of the former. (Many of the other patterns in this book can also be enlarged or reduced by either halving or doubling each line in the design.) Overall patterns with small shapes, like pattern II-8b, are particularly useful for upholstery to cover chairs and benches, since they can be cut off more or less arbitrarily and still look good.

Fig. 96. A sewn detail of the lower right-hand corner of pattern II-8a, worked in black, white, and three tones of gray. An interesting design will result if the entire pattern is colored according to this tonal arrangement.

Fig. 97. (Below) A larger portion of II-8a, worked by Carol DiSepio and colored differently than in Fig. 96. Here, the design is worked in two light shades of blue and one of green.

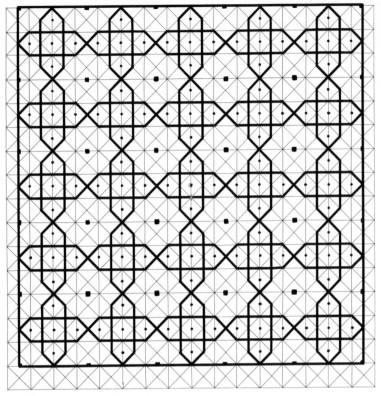

II-9 (Off-center pattern: see pages 70-71)

Pattern II-9

The arrangement of lines here produces two shapes: an eight-pointed star and a pointed cross. This configuration has fascinated designers throughout history, especially the Islamic craftsmen who used it repeatedly in their ceramic tile (Fig. 98), silk, and tapestry work. The eight-pointed star also appears as an element in Spanish, Italian, and Indian ornament.

This pattern struck me as especially beautiful when I saw it as a background decoration in an Indian miniature painting of the sixteenth century. The painting was called *Zardhank Khatini Brings the Ring to the Prison Keeper.* I colored it in my needlepoint as I had seen it in the painting (Fig. 99 and in color on page 159).

Stitching a triple outline like the one in Fig. 99 can be made easier by working the primary outline in one color (for example, white), and the rows to either side of it in a different but similar color (say, off-white). This will enable you to keep track of the primary outline as it interweaves throughout the design.

Fig. 98. A Persian ceramic tile of the thirteenth century, with the eight-pointed star configuration of pattern II-9. (The Metropolitan Museum of Art; Gift of Rafael Guastavino, 1928.)

Fig. 99.   A needlepoint pillow by Susan Schoenfeld, worked in red and green with the outline and dots in white. The linear aspect of the design is emphasized by stitching a triple outline. The small squares within the stars are each 5 by 5 stitches, with the center stitch of the square on the sixth thread of the unit. Each dot is a single stitch, also placed on the sixth thread of a unit.

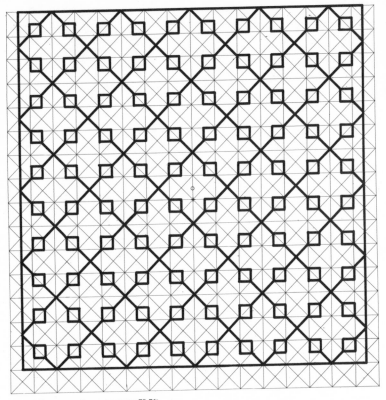

II-10 (Off-center pattern: see pages 70-71)

Pattern II-10

This design includes a variation of the pointed cross of the preceding pattern. The drawing is actually only the structural skeleton of an ornamental Indian design. Its full development occurs only when the pattern is worked as in Figs. 100 and 101.

Using the simple, linear structure which you have drawn on the canvas, outline the entire pattern, and fill in all the marked squares, with a medium-toned yarn. This done, follow the outline of each cross shape with a row of dark stitches next to the medium-toned row. Then place a row of light-toned stitches next to the dark row in each cross shape. Fill in the cross shapes with the dark color, leaving open one thread intersection for each white dot and nine thread intersections for each small white square shown in the photographs. Each dot is the ninth stitch from the point of an arm of the drawn cross shape. The small box in the center of each cross measures 3 stitches by 3 stitches and its center is the center of the cross shape drawn on the canvas. Fill in the dots and small boxes with white.

The symmetry which allows one to easily extend or reduce geometric patterns is evident in Fig. 101. This is one reason that such patterns appear throughout history in so many different uses and contexts.

Fig. 100.   A detail of the upper right-hand corner of pattern II-10, worked in four tones of gray from light to dark.

Fig. 101. Needlepoint piece in progress, worked on No. 10 mesh, by Pamela Patterson. The design measures 12 units by 12 units instead of the 15 by 15 units indicated in the drawing, and there are four repeats of the cross-shape rather than the five repeats included in the line drawing.

II-11

Pattern II-11

This handsome design combines the horizontal, vertical and diagonal lines of pattern sheet II with the curved shapes of pattern sheet IV. It was adapted from a carpet design in a fourteenth-century Persian miniature painting. It is a favorite of mine, because, although it is composed solely of regular geometric shapes, the imagery it produces is rich and varied, reminding me of leaves and flowers. The feeling of the pattern can be either bold or delicate, depending on the way in which it is colored. Figs. 102 (also color page 163) and 103 (see color page 162) show two quite different ways of coloring this design. For instructions on marking and stitching the circular outlines, see Chapter 8.

Fig. 102. Pattern II-11 made into a needlepoint pillow by Netty Barash. The pattern is expanded to form a rectangle by adding two repeats of the motif. Each repeat measures 6 by 6 units. The pillow is 20 by 14 inches, worked on No. 10 mono-mesh with Persian yarn. The outlines are worked in the same color as the background shapes (orange). The single stitches in the center of each floral shape has been expanded into a square measuring 3 by 3 stitches.

Fig. 103. Needlepoint by Betty Brean, worked on No. 10 penelope mesh with tapestry yarn. In this piece, the outlines are worked in the same color as the starlike center shape (beige).

86

Pattern II-12

This design, adapted from a Moorish tile pavement, is 20 by 20 units, too large to fit in its entirety on the pattern sheet. Therefore, one-quarter of the pattern is shown in the line drawing and the completed design is shown in Fig. 104. To draw the entire design, first draw a 20-inch by 20-inch square on the tracing paper and label each of the corners: bottom right, bottom left, top left and top right. Copy the design as it is shown in the drawing by placing the bottom-right corner of your 20-inch square at the bottom of the pattern sheet, a half-unit in from the right side, and copy the design as it is shown in the drawing. When you have completed this quarter of the tracing, revolve the paper and reposition it on the pattern sheet so that the top-right corner of your square is now aligned with the bottom of the pattern sheet, a half-unit in from the right side. Copy the line drawing as before.

Revolve the tracing paper clockwise twice more, putting each of the remaining two corners of your square at the bottom right of the pattern sheet in turn and copying the same lines as in the drawing. You need only revolve the tracing paper and reposition it on the pattern sheet to do this. Remember to begin a half-unit in from the right, because all the vertical lines fall on the half-units of the pattern sheet. The center of the design will be formed by the four quarters; although it does not match the center of the pattern sheet, it can be placed in the center of your canvas.

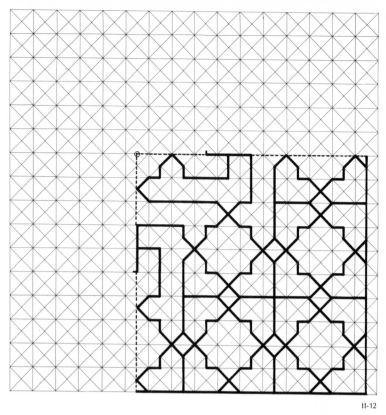

II-12

Fig. 104. A needlepoint of pattern II-12, to be made into a large pillow, by Susanna Briselli. This piece measures 20 inches square, worked on No. 10 mesh. Outlined in the lightest color. (Also shown on color page 162.)

II-13 (Off-center pattern: see pages 70-71)

Pattern II-13

Like pattern II-1, this also comes from the Alhambra. It is recommended for larger pieces of work, such as rugs, bench covers, screens, etc. (Fig. 105 and color page 157). Enough of the pattern is included in the line drawing for the entire repeat to be visible. In order to extend the design, copy the line drawing as given on a large sheet of tracing paper placed over the pattern sheet; then shift the tracing paper and continue drawing the pattern until you have included as many repeats as you will need to fit the required dimensions of your design.

Fig. 105. In this piece, designed by Winifred Bendiner and worked by Marie Love, pattern II-13 is used as the background for a figure based on pattern sheet IV (pattern IV-19). Some of the lines of pattern II-13 are omitted at the corners to make a more pleasing combined design for this bench cover.

Pattern II-14

This intricate Chinese lattice pattern can be designed for many uses and forms. The small overall pattern works well as upholstery, the intended use of the needlepoint in Fig. 106. The photograph shows one way to color the design; another way might be to retain the dark background and substitute dark but brilliant and jewel-like colors for the light and middle tones in the diamond shapes. A single pattern is rich in possibilities, and it will always look different, depending on the feelings and imagination of its designer.

II-14

Fig. 106. Needlepoint chair cover in progress, worked on No. 12 mono-mesh with tapestry yarn, by Sara Needle Eisenman. The background is dark blue-green; the diamonds are shades of yellow and rose. The outline is worked in pale yellow yarn.

II-15

Pattern II-15

This pattern is adapted from an Italian sixteenth-century pattern on silk damask. One can readily imagine its beauty and elegance in that monochromatic form, yet this is a pattern which may be colored successfully in many other ways. Fig. 107 shows one way; the photograph on page 174, in which the pattern is shown interpreted in patchwork, shows another.

Fig. 107. In this stitched portion of pattern II-15, the outlining is varied to enhance the decorative value. Some of the outlines are worked in dark, some in light, and some in middle-toned yarn, in a consistent pattern. This detail clearly shows the outlining pattern that is to be followed throughout the design. Each small square in the needlepoint is 3 by 3 stitches.

Pattern II-16

This pattern, which is taken from a Roman pavement design, is divided into 16 squares of 3 by 3 units. (The squares are formed by horizontal and vertical lines running the entire length and width of the pattern, which simplifies drawing and sewing the design.) Once the pattern has been divided into these 16 squares, the shapes that fall within them can be more easily placed.

This pattern and the next four, which follow the same principle, are especially suitable for rugs and other large pieces. You can extend the design by simply repeating as many squares as you wish. To simplify handling designs larger than 24 inches square, you may work additional repeats on separate pieces of canvas, which may then be sewn together.

II-16

Fig. 108. A detail of the upper right-hand corner of pattern II-16 (one-quarter of the entire design). The shapes are worked to look as if transparent colors were superimposed; the darkest shape (blue) is "overlaid" with a yellow shape, which, when "mixed" with the blue, produces a middle-tone green (the center shape). The light background tone is off-white. The straight lines which run the length and width of the pattern are worked with black yarn; all other outlines are orange.

Pattern II-17

This pattern is derived from Chinese lattice work. It is divided into 64 small squares and 16 large ones (of 4 by 4 units). Two configurations alternate within the large squares. These different configurations are created by the arrangement of only three shapes within each small square: a one-unit square and two trapezoids. In the needlepoint design in Fig. 109, an irregular hexagon is formed because some of the trapezoids have been worked in the same dark color as the outlining.

II-18

Pattern II-18

Another lattice pattern, this is also divided into 16 large squares of 4 by 4 units. Each square contains the same configuration shown in the sewn detail (Fig. 110), but in alternate squares the image is reversed as in a mirror. Repeating the tonal arrangement of Fig. 110 in the other squares will achieve a kaleidoscopic effect, so that the finished design will look completely different than the single motif which produced it.

Fig. 109. Needlepoint pillow designed by Winifred Bendiner; worked by Mae Eisenberg, in shades of green and off-white.

Fig. 110. A sewn detail of the square in the lower right-hand corner of pattern II-18. The outline is worked with white yarn, and filled in with black, three tones of gray, and ecru.

II-19

Pattern II-19

This is based on a German parquet-floor pattern. In the original, each shape would have been an inlaid piece of wood. The individual pieces would be assembled into squares and used to cover an entire floor. This illustrates the special usefulness of these patterns. Just as the German floor-makers might fit this design to any room by using a greater or lesser number of parquet blocks, you may design with a greater or lesser number of needlepoint squares. You may even take only one line of squares and use it as a band or border.

Fig. 111. A sewn detail of the lower right-hand corner of pattern II-19. It is worked in black, white, ecru (the large triangles), and three tones of gray. This interesting pattern allows for varied experimentation and interpretation.

Pattern II-20

Another German parquet pattern, this is made up of only three shapes. Because of the particular arrangement of the shapes, the pattern represents a wide range of options for designing with color and tone. (See Fig. 112 and color page 164.) Try doing small sketches of it, by tracing directly from the line drawing, and then color the sketches in to see how many different designs you can create.

II-20

Fig. 112. Needlepoint pillow, designed by Winifred Bendiner and worked by Elinor Migdal. Based on pattern II-20, this is 18 inches square, worked on No. 10 mesh with tapestry yarn. The border is colored differently than the center of the design. The pillow is finished with antique fringes and crocheted balls. (See patchwork pattern 2, page 187.)

II-21 (Off-center pattern: see pages 70-71)

Pattern II-21

The following five patterns (II-21 through II-25) all include eight-sided figures. In order to give the largest and most pleasing repeat of these patterns, they are all made up of an odd number of units and therefore are off-center on the pattern sheet.

For the first of these patterns, we go to the well once more: the Alhambra, fortress-palace of the Moorish kings at Granada, Spain, which is so rich in mosaic tile patterns. In this pattern, the octagons are enclosed by irregular hexagons and small diamond shapes (Fig. 113).

Fig. 113. Needlepoint pillow by Doris Gluck, 14 units square, with a border of narrow stripes, worked on No. 10 penelope mesh with tapestry yarn. The octagons and the outlines are in the same color (the lightest tone).

Pattern II-22

In this Arabian floor pattern, the octagons enclose alternating horizontal and vertical rectangles, which gives an added rhythmic feeling to the design. Small diamonds are formed between adjacent octagons (Fig. 114).

II-22 (Off-center pattern: see pages 70-71)

Fig. 114.   A sewn detail of the upper right-hand corner of pattern II-22. Here the outline is identical to the light background, and therefore disappears.

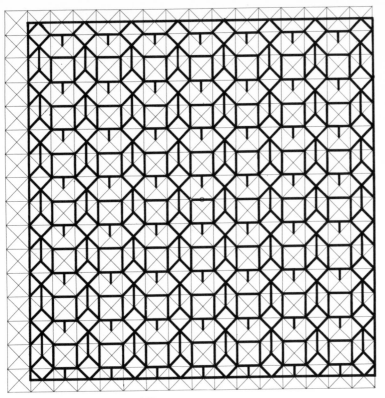

II-23 (Off-center pattern: see pages 70-71)

Pattern II-23

This pattern and the following one are related; they both appear in ornamental designs of the European Middle Ages. In Fig. 115, the design is shaded to give it a three-dimensional effect and the octagons seem to be threaded in vertical rows on a black string. The basic configuration is actually the same as in the preceding pattern (II-22); instead of enclosing rectangles, here each octagon encloses two parallelograms, a square, and an irregular hexagon.

Fig. 115. Needlepoint pillow designed by Susan Schoenfeld and worked by Elinor Migdal in black, white, three tones of gray, and dark red. The pattern is outlined in a middle tone, which is also used to fill in the square shapes. One stitch on the bottom row of each square is left blank to accommodate the short black lines, each of which extends five more stitches in length. The striped border alternates two rows of a dark with one row of a light tone.

Pattern II-24

In this pattern, squares and irregular hexagons combine to form interlocked octagons. The design is embellished with single lines, each one unit long horizontally or vertically, which form crosses at the points of the hexagons. The decorative effect created by such lines can be adapted to many other patterns based on pattern sheets II and IV, by placing crossed lines at selected points in the design. If you choose a complex color arrangement in working this pattern, you may wish to omit the crossed lines to avoid a too-busy design (Fig. 116).

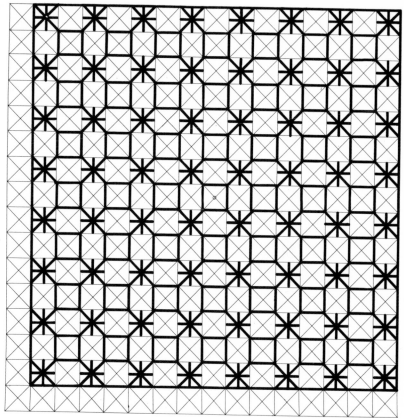

II-24 (Off-center pattern: see pages 70-71)

Fig. 116. Needlepoint piece by Yetta Kalish, worked on No. 10 mono-mesh with Persian yarn. Some of the textured effect of this piece was created by replacing one of the three strands of Persian yarn with a strand of another color, and using this "mixed" yarn to fill in a shape. (See color page 161.)

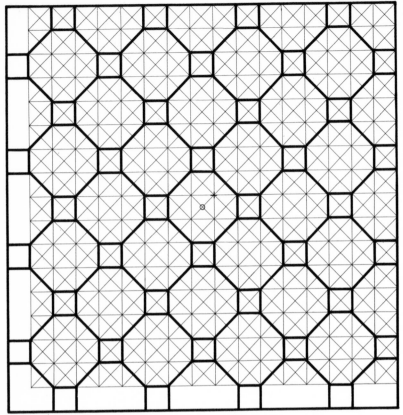

II-25 (Off-center pattern: see pages 70-71)

Pattern II-25

This basic octagonal configuration is given one unit larger than the pattern sheet to accommodate four repeats horizontally and vertically. It is a bare structure of a pattern, and for that very reason it is versatile and can be applied to a number of design uses. In Fig. 117, the structural outline is emphasized, and a varied and decorative pattern of color and tone is applied, keeping the octagons two constant colors and making the squares three additional colors (see color page 161).

Other ways of embellishing this kind of structural pattern can be found in different examples of decorative art. Figs. 118 and 119 both show Japanese textiles that use this octagonal configuration as a basic structure for elaborate counter-patterning. (Some of the patterns given in this book can be found within the octagons and squares in Fig. 119.)

Fig. 117. Needlepoint designed by Winifred Bendiner and worked by Mollie Heller, on No. 12 mesh (making the piece approximately 14 inches square). Here the outlines of the octagons are echoed and made into a decorative element. Starting from the outline in the line drawing, which is worked in dark yarn, four extra rows are worked within the octagon shape only, in this sequence: light, dark, light, dark.

Fig. 118. In this Japanese kimono, the octagon pattern is used to enclose simple floral shapes and more intricate arabesques. (The Metropolitan Museum of Art, Bequest of Edward C. Moore, 1891.)

Fig. 119. In this piece of Japanese brocade, the octagon pattern is used both to enclose other patterns *and* as a background for the superimposed dragons. (The Metropolitan Museum of Art, Gift of Mr. and Mrs. H. O. Havemeyer, 1896.)

A

B

C

D

II-26

Pattern II-26

Here are four band and/or border designs. Although many of the designs already given can become band or border designs, these are especially well-fitted to this purpose. Pattern **A** is a ribbon-like configuration containing squares of 3 by 3 units (Fig. 121). Patterns **B** and **C** are variations of each other; they alternate whole and divided squares (Figs. 120 and 122). Pattern **D** is a larger design. Except in larger pieces, such as a rug, it is more suitable for use as a band than as a border. Patterns like this can be used to make bellpulls or wall hangings.

Fig. 120. Sewn detail of band **B**, in black, white, and two tones of gray.

Fig. 121. Sewn detail of band **A**. Major parts are outlined in dark yarn, and the background triangles are filled in with the same color; vertical and horizontal outlines within the major shapes are worked in a light-middle tone, and remaining areas are filled in to create stripes of light, middle, and dark tones.

Fig. 122. Sewn detail of band **C**, in black, white, and two tones of gray.

102

Pattern II-27

Some people love knots, puzzles, riddles, and conundrums; others are frustrated by them. If you find them fascinating, you will probably enjoy working this knot of interlocking square and rectangular links. It opens up the possibility of making each link a different color, either using a neutral sewn outline for all, or outlining each link in the color yarn with which it is to be filled in.

II-27

Pattern II-28

This design, adapted from Victorian English patchwork, also makes a fine border for needlepoint (also see the needlepoint border on page 155). The shapes in this pattern can be enlarged for use in patchwork (see Chapter 10).

II-28

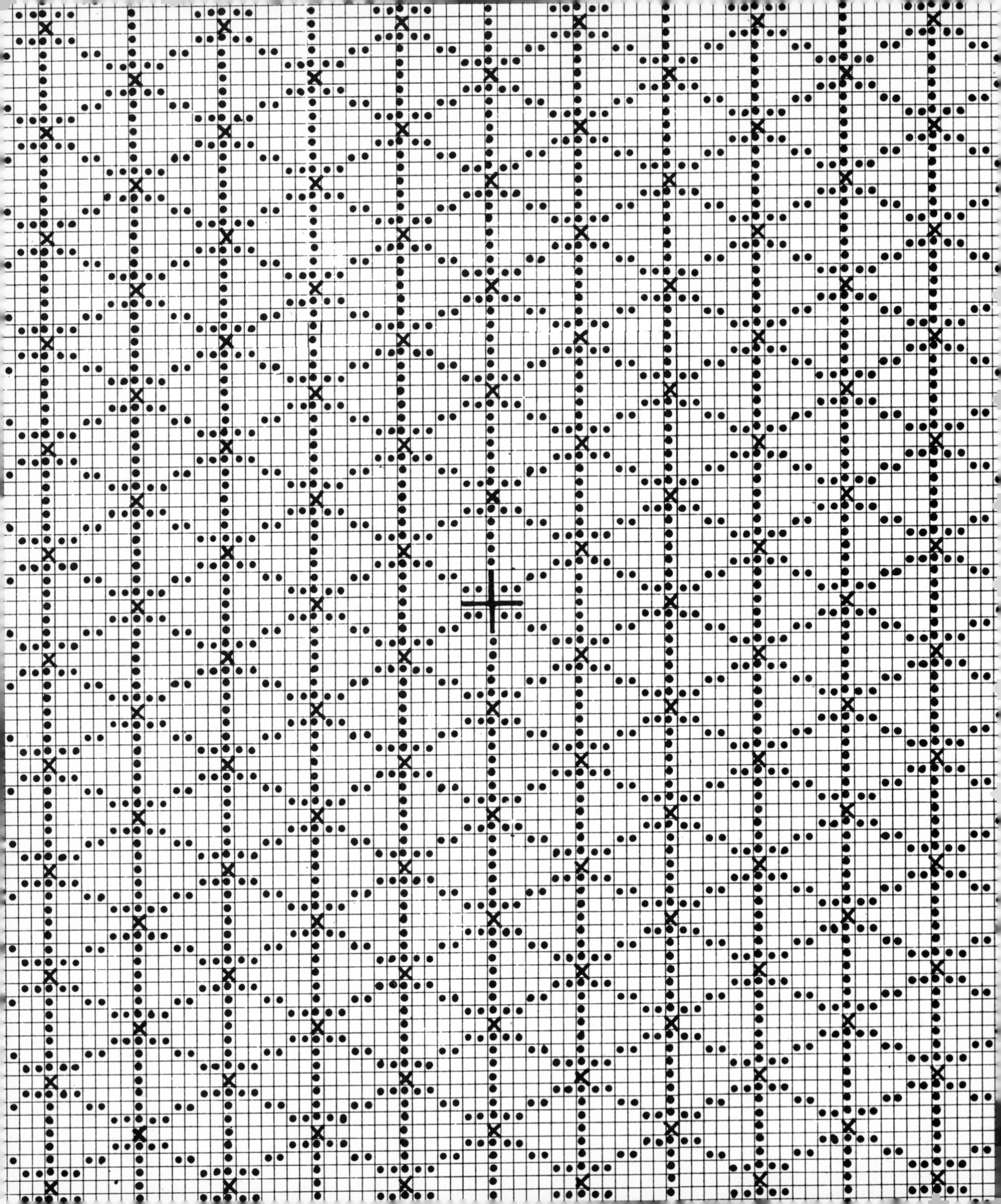

7. Pattern Sheet III: The Equilateral Triangle

Fig. 123. (Opposite page) Part of pattern sheet III.

It seems appropriate that the third pattern sheet is concerned with a three-sided figure, and this chapter examines the ramifications of using this special, almost magical figure for pattern design. The equilateral triangle has been used throughout history for its design and structural qualities; it is in fact the basis of many architectural achievements, including Buckminster Fuller's innovative geodesic domes. The fact that its three sides are equal is the key to this triangle's utility for our design purposes as well.

The equal, triangular shapes on this pattern sheet are, in effect, the "alphabet" of the designs in this chapter. How these basic units combine to form such a variety of designs is almost as astonishing as how the 26 letters of the alphabet combine to form so many different words (Fig. 124). Like words, shapes can also express feeling and ideas. It is a curious fact that while Western design has favored four-sided figures, the East has historically leaned toward the three-sided figure, reflecting a different view of the order of the universe.

Fig. 124. Equilateral triangles combine to form a wide variety of design shapes.

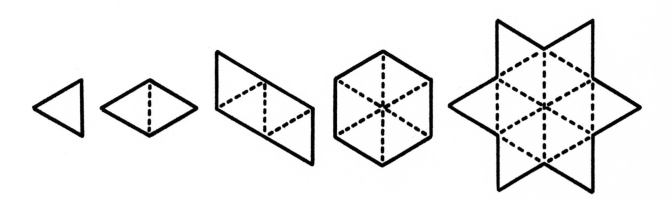

Measuring, Marking, and Stitching

The basic units of this pattern sheet then are the equilateral triangles formed by a network of dotted vertical and opposing diagonal lines. These diagonals are equally spaced parallel lines drawn at a 60° angle to the vertical in opposite directions. The diagonal lines alone form a network of equal-sided parallelograms. The vertical lines divide the parallelograms into equilateral triangles. Each intersection of a diagonal with a vertical is marked with an **X** and these are also the points where opposing diagonals meet.

Looking at this network of lines you can see that the diagonals and verticals form many other shapes in addition to the small triangles. Diamonds, hexagons, six-pointed stars, and chevrons can all be discerned and constructed by selecting and emphasizing various combinations of lines on the pattern sheet. As the designs in this chapter rely on the linear structure provided by the diagonal and vertical lines of the pattern sheet, all units are measure *inclusively* from **X** to **X**, so that the boundaries of the shapes may be outlined. Like the designs based on pattern sheet II, the linear aspects of these designs may be either stressed or obscured by your selection of outlining colors.

Each basic equilateral triangle measures 9 boxes vertically and 8 boxes along its diagonal sides. (The linear measurements of all three sides are equal even though there are fewer boxes covered diagonally.) All boxes, and therefore the threads and stitches, are counted inclusively from **X** to **X** (Fig. 125). Although there are no horizontal lines on this pattern sheet, you can see that two **X**'s can be connected horizontally and that there are 15 boxes counted inclusively from **X** to **X**. This is the horizontal measurement of the pattern sheet and it is used for sectioning off the horizontal center line of the canvas. The vertical measurement from **X** to **X** is 9.

Fig. 125. Each equilateral triangle measures 9 boxes vertically and 8 boxes along its diagonal sides. All boxes, and therefore threads and stitches, are counted inclusively from **X** to **X**. The 15 boxes counted inclusively from **X** to **X** across the graph paper is the horizontal measure of this pattern sheet.

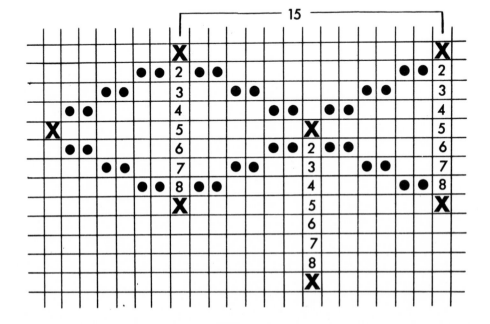

Like the vertical lines in pattern sheet II, the vertical lines here are also marked *on* the threads of the canvas. The diagonals, however, unlike those of the previous two pattern sheets based on the square format of the canvas itself, cannot be marked in a straight path on the intersections of the canvas threads. It is therefore necessary to count, mark, and stitch these diagonals in a different way (Figs. 126, 127, and 128).

In Fig. 126, you can see that the diagonals appear as stepped lines with two dots for each step between every two **X**'s, so that each diagonal may be counted inclusively from **X** to **X** in the following sequence: one—two—two—two—one; and this count is repeated along the entire diagonal. The same counting sequence is used to mark the proper thread intersections of the canvas and to sew the stitches along the desired diagonal path. This means that you begin a diagonal line with a single stitch at one **X**, sew three groups of double stitches placed side by side, then place a single stitch at the next **X**, and continue—either along the same diagonal or along the opposing diagonal—with another trio of double stitches placed side by side. This sequence of eight stitches may be used for a diagonal of any length in either direction provided you begin and end with a single stitch at each **X**.

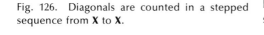

Fig. 126. Diagonals are counted in a stepped sequence from **X** to **X**.

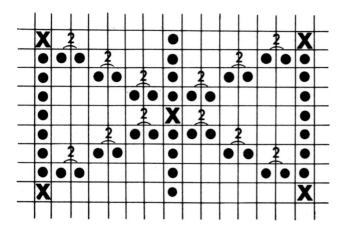

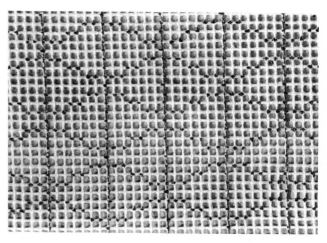

Fig. 127. Vertical lines are marked on the threads of the canvas; diagonal lines are marked on the thread intersections in the same sequence by which the boxes are counted.

Fig. 128. The outlines marked on the canvas become sewn boundaries between adjacent shapes. Diagonals are stitched with the one–two–two–two–one sequence and may be worked up or down the canvas. (The sequence must be worked from right to left when going up the canvas, but may be worked from left to right as well when going down the canvas.)

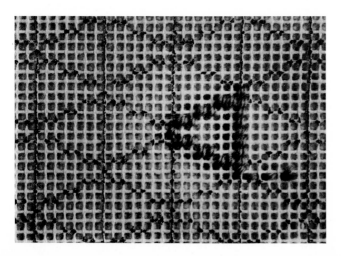

107

The designs are traced in the same way as the previous ones, by following the contours outlined in the drawing and marking them in enlarged form on tracing paper placed over the pattern sheet. With only four exceptions, no horizontal lines are used in these designs.

In transferring the design to canvas, the center rules are drawn first, *on* the threads of the canvas. The vertical line is sectioned off into units of 9 threads, counted inclusively, with each unit marked *on* the ninth horizontal thread. The horizontal line is sectioned off into units of 15, counted inclusively, with the units marked on every fifteenth vertical thread (Fig. 129). It is not necessary to mark the horizontal rule into smaller units. Whenever a vertical line of the design does not fall on the first or fifteenth thread, it will always fall on the eighth thread of a unit. If the diagonal sequence is correctly counted and marked, the vertical lines will fall into place automatically (Fig. 130).

If you wish to know how many stitches (or threads) are needed for a vertical line covering more than one unit, multiply the number of units it covers on the pattern sheet by 8 and add 1. A vertical line covering two units requires 17 stitches ($8 \times 2 + 1$). The diagonals are always marked

Fig. 129. Center guide lines are sectioned off into groups of 9 threads along the vertical line and groups of 15 threads along the horizontal line. All lines are marked on the threads.

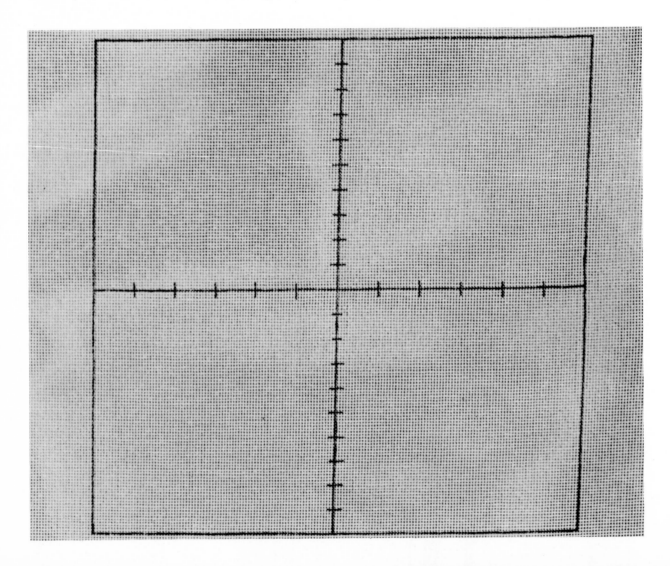

and stitched in the eight-count sequence already described. But if you wish to check the total number of stitches (or threads) needed for a diagonal line extending over more than one unit, multiply the number of units it covers by 7 and add 1. A diagonal line covering two units requires 15 stitches ($7 \times 2 + 1$). The maximum vertical measurement of the pattern sheet is 161 stitches (20 units high $\times$ 8 + 1). The maximum diagonal measurement of the pattern sheet is 169 stitches (24 units $\times$ 7 + 1), which is also the maximum horizontal measurement.

As with pattern sheet II, all the outlines of the designs are worked first. All the vertical lines are worked with the vertical variation of the continental stitch described in Chapter 2, and the diagonal lines are worked with the stitch sequence described in this chapter. Any horizontal lines you wish to add can be marked on the threads of the canvas and worked as described in Chapter 2. The shapes are then filled in with the basket weave stitch, with separate tent stitches added where needed. Again, the outlines can be stressed by working the shapes in a contrasting color, or the shapes themselves may be stressed by working them in the same color as the defining outlines.

Fig. 130.   Design from pattern sheet III marked on the canvas.

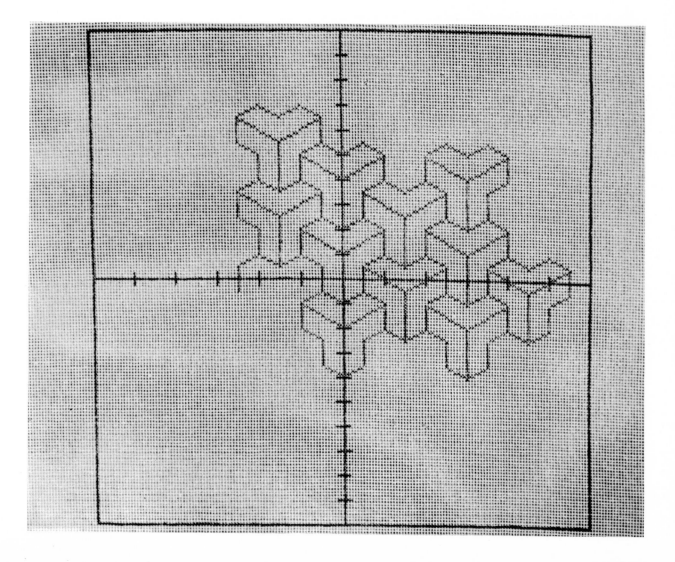

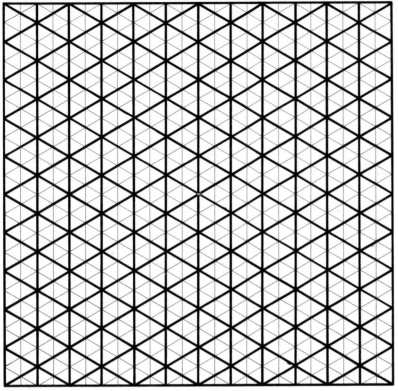

III-1

Pattern III-1

This first pattern simply shows the pattern sheet itself enlarged, illustrating how any pattern, not only in this chapter but throughout the book, may be enlarged by multiplying each line a uniform number of units. A basic pattern such as this poses many possibilities even without further refinement.

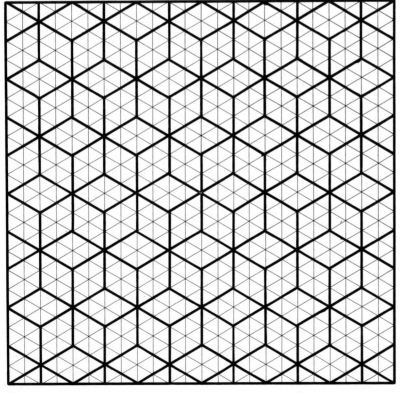

III-2

Pattern III-2

If there existed such a thing as a roster of all-time most popular patterns, this one would be on it. Called "Baby's Blocks" in patchwork, this pattern is ecumenical enough to have been a Chinese wedding-coat design, and timely enough to resemble present-day *trompe d'oeil* painting (Fig. 132). (See color page 164.)

Fig. 131. One possibility for coloring pattern III-1. Here the dark and middle-toned triangles are arranged in diagonal rows, with the light triangles filling the spaces between.

Fig. 132. Small needlepoint pillow by Winifred Bendiner, worked on No. 12 mesh with tapestry yarn. The coloring of the diamond shapes in this design creates a random pattern of light-and-dark cube shapes. If you wish to strengthen the optical illusion, you can tone the shapes in a more consistent manner, keeping the tops of the cube shapes a middle tone, each right side light and each left side dark.

III-3

Pattern III-3

This Japanese triple-diamond design, said to have been derived from the look of pine-tree bark, can be used well to enclose smaller designs within the large shapes (see page 144). Or, the pattern could serve as a background for a central motif taken from another pattern in this chapter, as pattern II-13 was used with pattern IV-19 (see page 88).

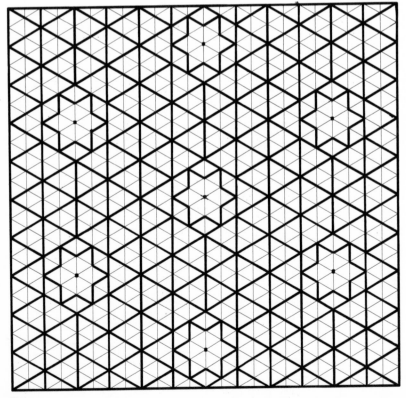

III-4

Pattern III-4

Compare this pattern to the first one in this chapter, and you will see how closely they are related. In fact, they are exactly the same with the sole exception of the six-pointed stars enclosed within hexagons. Six-pointed stars are an important part of the vocabulary of these patterns. The hexagons which enclose these stars can themselves be seen to be the centers of still larger six-pointed stars.

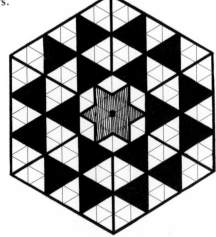

Pattern III-5

Composed solely of six-pointed stars, this design appears in a silk brocade woven in the thirteenth or fourteenth century by Chinese craftsmen. The points of the stars touch in a manner that also creates small diamonds and encloses each star in a hexagon.

The pattern is shown slightly smaller than the pattern sheet to make a more visually satisfying cutoff. Each square in the center of a star is 3 stitches by 3 stitches.

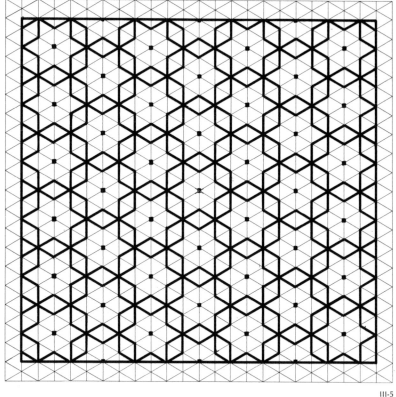

III-5

Fig. 133. A sewn portion of pattern III-5. The overall pattern of stars is emphasized by stitching those shapes in the same light color as the outline.

Fig. 134. Needlepoint designed by Winifred Bendiner and worked by Doris Gluck. This pillow, using only a portion of the design, measures approximately 11 by 14 inches, worked on No. 10 mesh with tapestry yarn. The seven stars worked with dark yarn create a focus at the center. (See color page 161.)

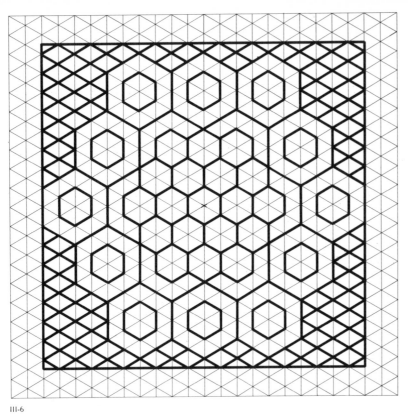

III-6

Pattern III-6

The regular hexagon is one of the most basic shapes formed on this pattern sheet. It is one of the richer geometric forms used for pattern designing, one of the few which can be placed together in an overall pattern with no space being left between (a natural efficiency which is used to advantage even by bees, whose honeycombs are made up of perfect hexagons).

Two sewn details (Figs. 135 and 136) isolate two elements of the design: simple, adjacent hexagons, and hexagons enclosed within larger hexagons. Either of these elements could be used as a separate pattern. The hexagon is a shape which can easily be expanded to double, triple, quadruple its size or larger. In fact, it can be expanded to become the outside dimensions of the design itself (see patterns III-20 and 21).

Fig. 135. (Above) A sewn portion of pattern based on a network of hexagons. This design, when repeated, will create six light hexagons surrounding a single dark one.

Fig. 136. A network of larger hexagons with smaller hexagons placed within them.

Fig. 137. Needlepoint pillow designed by Winifred Bendiner and worked by Roberta Shapiro; approximately 14 inches square, worked on No. 10 mesh with tapestry yarn. Small light and dark diamonds create an attractive background for the hexagon design, making a border unnecessary. The background diamond pattern could be extended to make a larger piece of work. (See color page 161.)

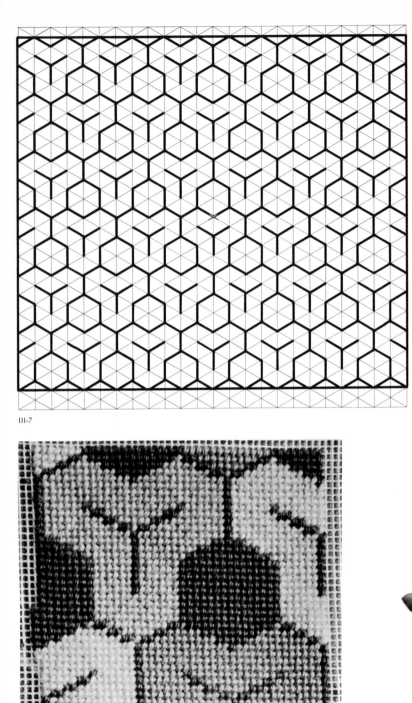

III-7

Pattern III-7

This pattern is made up entirely of hexagons; the "Y" shapes are formed by three adjoining hexagons whose common boundaries have been left out. The linear "Y"s are the boundaries of two other hexagons whose remaining sides are not delineated. This is a Japanese design, called the "tortoise shell" pattern, symbolizing long life and good luck.

Fig. 139. (Above) Hexagons, diamonds, and Y-shapes are interspersed with the figurative images of birds, clouds, flowers, and dragons in this nineteenth-century Japanese robe. (The Metropolitan Museum of Art, Fletcher Fund, 1935.)

Fig. 138. A portion of pattern III-7 worked in four tones. The outlines (including the linear "Y"s) are worked in the same color as that used to fill in the hexagons.

Pattern III-8

This design, based on Russian ornament, takes the "tortoise shell" pattern one step further. The linear "Y"'s are extended to touch the three corners of the "Y" shapes, forming V-like configurations, which are the only shapes in the design.

III-8

Fig. 140. A portion of pattern III-8 worked in dark, light, and middle tones, and outlined in the middle tone. Coloring the "V" shapes in this way creates a three-dimensional illusion similar to the shaded cubes in pattern III-2.

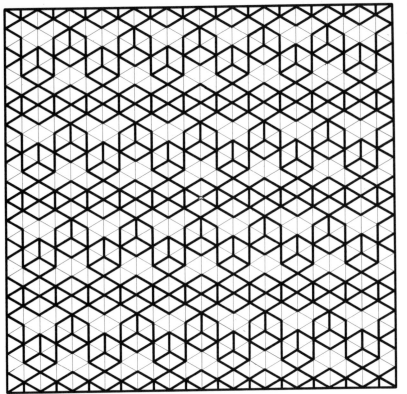

III-9

Pattern III-9

An intriguing pattern based on small diamond shapes. When this pattern is colored as in Fig. 141, two distinct configurations are produced: three-dimensional cubes, and a pattern of dark and light diamonds. The remaining middle-toned, ten-sided figures function as a rest area between those two active elements. This design can be used as an overall pattern, as in the line drawing, or, since the pattern arranges itself into bands, it can be easily adapted to belts, borders, etc.

Fig. 141. A portion of pattern III-9 worked in five tones. The outline is worked in the next-to-the-darkest tone (the same as that used to fill in the tops of the cube shapes).

Pattern III-10

This pattern of chevrons is quite serviceable for use as a background with another design superimposed over it, as a border, or in its own right as a design. The pattern is produced by interlocking hexagons, with one of the six sides undelineated.

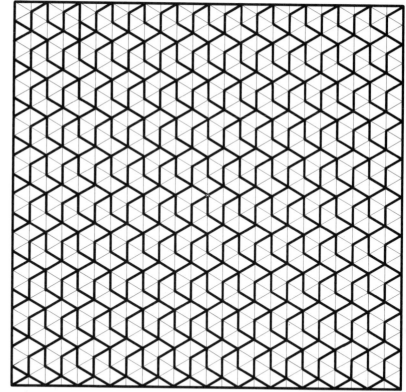

III-10

Fig. 142. A portion of pattern III-10 worked in three tones. The chevrons are filled in with relatively dark and light tones; the outline is a neutral, middle tone which falls between them.

III-11

Pattern III-11

This pattern, like the previous one, can be seen as interlocking hexagons, with three rather than one side missing (or it can be seen as zigzag lines which run in three directions). When worked, none of the shapes in the design should be filled in with the same color as the outline, because patterns like this, and the previous one as well, depend for their effect on all shapes being the same size.

Fig. 143. A portion of pattern III-11 worked in four tones. For coloring suggestion, see the macramé-fringed work on color page 160.

Pattern III-12

This pattern, which resembles interwoven caning, appears in a fifteenth-century Persian miniature now in the Metropolitan Museum of Art (Fig. 144). In the sewn detail (Fig. 145), the outline is the same color as the hexagons. Another way to design it might be to make the outline a color which is not repeated elsewhere in the design. This would allow you to vary the color of the hexagons. In either case the interwoven bands formed by the parallelograms could all be made a single color, as shown in Fig. 145, or in varied colors to stress the effect of long strips woven together.

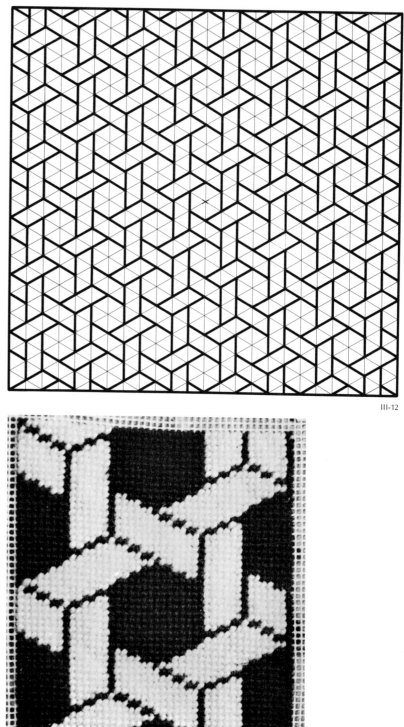

III-12

Fig. 144. Persian miniature paintings are a rich source of decorative geometric patterns, used in elaborate backgrounds. This painting of the seventeenth century contains more than a dozen different patterns. (The Metropolitan Museum of Art, Fletcher Fund, 1963.)

Fig. 145. A portion of pattern III-12 worked in two tones.

121

III-13

Pattern III-13

This pattern seems to present a hexagon which is imprisoned within two interlocking triangular bands. Its origin is an Indian window-lattice pattern. You may color each of the triangular bands autonomously, which will serve to emphasize the effect of interlocking links.

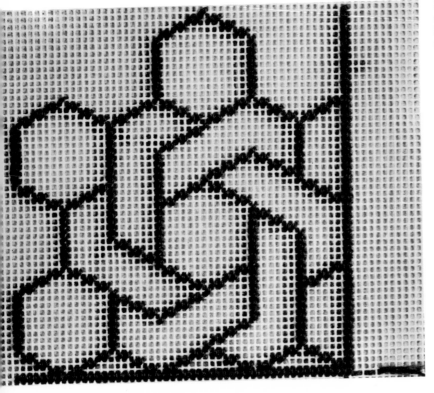

Fig. 146. Stitched outline of the lower right-hand corner of pattern III-13. Here you can clearly see how the stitch sequence for pattern sheet III delineates the shapes of the pattern.

Pattern III-14

This pattern, like the preceding one, originated as an Indian window-lattice design. It carries the idea advanced in the previous two patterns (straight-line shapes surrounding hexagons) still further. In this pattern, the straight-line shapes do not interlock or weave; rather they appear as "V" shapes which seem to float in space. This opens up other coloring possibilities, two of which are illustrated here (Figs. 147 and 148).

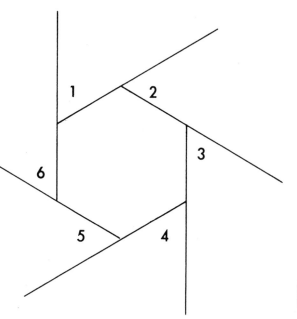

III-14

Fig. 147. Taking the hexagon as the center, the "V" shapes surrounding it are colored in a circular sequence. Here, each "V" is a different color. If this arrangement is repeated throughout the design, no two "V"'s of the same color will touch.

Fig. 148. Needlepoint pillow designed and worked by Howard Kalish. The outline and the hexagons are worked in the same color yarn (white). The surrounding "V"'s are worked in a circular sequence of three colors, with a second sequence of three additional colors used on the shapes surrounding the hexagons in alternate horizontal rows. (See color page 157.)

Pattern III-15

This pattern is another variation on the theme created in the preceding patterns, from the same source. Here "A" shapes revolve about six-pointed stars, which can be seen either as the figure or the ground. When worked, the outline should be in a different color than any of the "A" shapes; it can be in the same color as the small triangles or the stars, or it can simply be a color that does not reappear in the design. One way to insure that no two "A" shapes of the same color will touch is to color them alternately throughout the pattern, like a checkerboard. (The alternate colors need not be light and dark; they may be similar tones but of different hues.)

Pattern III-16

I affectionately call this pattern "running things," for reasons which are apparent. The "running things" are self-contained shapes set upon a ground which is connected throughout the pattern. Patterns with larger shapes, such as this one and the preceding one, are especially suitable for rugs or other large pieces of work; simply extend the given pattern to the desired dimensions.

Pattern III-17

The name of this Japanese design means "leaves of the hemp plant." Originally a design on an ancient Buddhist image, it became popular in Japan as a pattern for babies' kimonos. Parents hoped that infants wearing it would develop the vigor and toughness of the hemp plant.

In order to work this pattern, and the next two, you will need to use another sequence of stitches, in addition to the standard one for this pattern sheet. These patterns contain lines moving from **X** to **X** along an unmarked diagonal (Fig. 149). In order to mark and sew this line, count thirteen thread intersections inclusively from **X** to **X** in the sequence shown by Fig. 150. This sequence crosses two equilateral triangles; to cross four triangles, count the sequence twice.

III-17

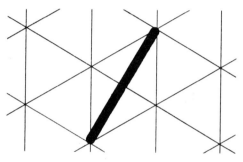

Fig. 149. Lines of design move from **X** to **X** on a different diagonal than those of the pattern sheet.

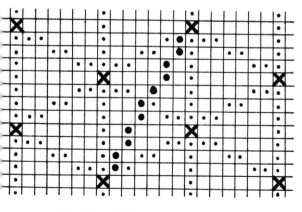

Fig. 150. Stitch sequence for this diagonal.

Fig. 151. A portion of pattern III-17 worked in five tones (including the outline tone, which is not used to fill in any of the shapes). A familiar six-pointed star (often used in Christmas decorations) appears when this photograph is turned sideways. This star can be made more prominent by coloring the triangles within it alternately dark and light against a middle-toned background. The linear quality of the original design may be stressed by outlining the entire pattern in a dark color and filling in each shape with a light color.

125

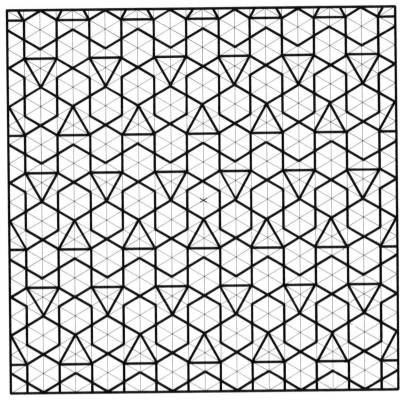

III-18

Pattern III-18

This pattern derives from one in a Persian miniature painting called *Firdowsi's Parable of the Ship of Shi'ism*, by Mirza Ali (sixteenth century). It is shown made into a handbag (Fig. 152). Patterns having small repeats such as this one are well adapted to this use. They are easily cropped to smaller or odd sizes, while still remaining visually satisfying.

In Fig. 152, the hexagons are colored in horizontal bands, in varying tones of gray; the remaining shapes are consistently a dark and very light gray. (See color page 157.) The zigzag boundaries of the shapes define the lower edge of the flap. This flap is made by clipping the unworked mesh at the inner and outer points of the shapes, turning it back and gluing it to the wrong side of the work. The sides and bottom of the handbag are made from a band of hexagons worked in a vertical row.

Fig. 152. (Left) A small handbag made in three pieces, with a chain for a handle. Designed and worked by Susan Schoenfeld, on No. 12 mesh with tapestry yarn.

Fig. 153. (Above) A variation on the coloring idea which appears in the handbag. In both designs, the outline is the same color as the triangle, but here the star-shape becomes more prominent.

Pattern III-19

This design of overlapping rectangles which tumble about a hexagon is derived from one carved in plaster in a Mogul palace of the sixteenth century. In the coloring of the sewn work, the idea of superimposing "transparent" colors is investigated (Fig. 154). Patterns which, in line, suggest overlapping shapes can be colored to accentuate the overlap. If the rectangles which overlap in this pattern were made of a transparent material, such as panes of colored glass, the smaller shapes which are common to two of them would be darker than either. This effect of nature is imitated in coloring the design.

In doing color sketches of this pattern, it can be especially helpful and interesting to experiment with watercolors on heavy tracing paper or vellum. Having drawn the design in pencil, color a rectangle with watercolor. Wait for the paint to dry, and then color an overlapping rectangle with another color. A third color will be produced where the two rectangles overlap.

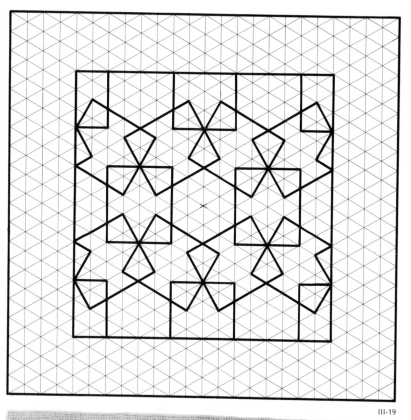

III-19

Fig. 154. Needlepoint designed by Howard Kalish and worked by Herta Bilus, on No. 10 mesh with tapestry yarn. In this pattern, the outline color should not be the same as that of any of the shapes, so that it can be distinctly visible throughout the design. Eighteen different colors are used in this needlepoint piece. (See color page 163.)

III-20

Pattern III-20

This hexagonal design, which stems from Chinese lattice-work, is shown made into a box pillow (Fig. 155). It is sewn in three primary colors, each going from light to dark in eight steps from center. The gray hexagon in the center is the same color as the outline. (See color page 158.)

The sides of the box pillow are worked as one long band on a separate piece of canvas equaling the length of the hexagon's perimeter. The design on the band is made up of nine vertical bars (each bar is nine stitches wide counted inclusively) for each side of the hexagon. The band is also outlined in gray and filled in with the same colors as the face of the pillow.

Fig. 155. Box pillow by Susan Schoenfeld, on No. 10 mesh with tapestry yarn.

Pattern III-21

Rather than being a basic kind of pattern with parts that can easily be moved about, this is an enclosed design in which the parts are brought to a more-or-less immutable balance. This is an adaptation of a mosaic-tile floor pavement design. Its relative immutability extends also to the coloring (see page 162); that is, the hues may be changed, but the dark-and-light value relationships should remain as shown in Fig. 156.

III-21

Fig. 156.   Needlepoint pillow designed by Susan Schoenfeld and worked by Nancy Finkelstein, on No. 12 mesh. When working this design, it is important to keep track of the tonal arrangement of the diamond shapes within the interwoven six-pointed star; if this pattern is not followed, the design will become confusing.

129

III-22

Pattern III-22

This figure appears to be going first in one direction and then another and gives the effect of an optical illusion.

If you wish to make the border shown in the sewn work (Fig. 157), you can follow the drawing to trace the hexagons in the top and bottom margins; in order to fill in the hexagons in the side margins, you must turn your traced drawing around 90° so those areas are at the top and bottom of the pattern sheet. You can then follow the line drawing as before. (Be sure to place the inside lines of the borders you have already drawn for the top and bottom on the vertical lines of the pattern sheet, so you can draw the hexagons outward from those lines. The outside lines of the top and bottom borders, which are now at the left and right of the pattern sheet, should not be aligned with any drawn verticals on the pattern sheet.)

Mark the top and bottom borders on the canvas in the usual way. Before marking the side borders, mark an extra horizontal thread at the bottom of the top squares and at the top of the bottom squares. You may then mark the hexagons of the side borders; but note that the stitch sequence for these diagonals will have the pairs of stitches placed together vertically instead of horizontally and will connect horizontal lines of the design rather than vertical ones. (See page 107; turn Fig. 126, which shows the normal stitch sequence, 90° and you will see the sequence used for the side borders.) The canvas is not turned; the stitch sequence is. The extra row of stitches added to each square compensates for the rectangular shape of the pattern sheet and allows the hexagons in the side borders to come out the same as those in the top and bottom.

Fig. 157. Needlepoint pillow by Sandra Roth, worked on No. 10 mesh with tapestry yarn. The entire design is outlined with black yarn; the central design is worked in white, rose, and two tones of brown, on a yellow background; the border is worked in two tones of blue on a black background, with corner squares worked in a purple-pink.

Pattern III-23

This pattern and the following one are Japanese emblem designs. Each can appear either as a flat, linear figure on a ground, or as a three-dimensional boxlike configuration.

This first one, which I have nicknamed "Baby Sam's Block," is colored in the example on page 158 to reinforce the three-dimensional imagery of a cube floating in space.

III-23

Pattern III-24

This design reads as a puzzle or knot. One suggestion for coloring it is to treat each of the three main portions of the design as the shaded side of a cube seen in perspective, creating a three-dimensional effect as in the previous design.

III-24

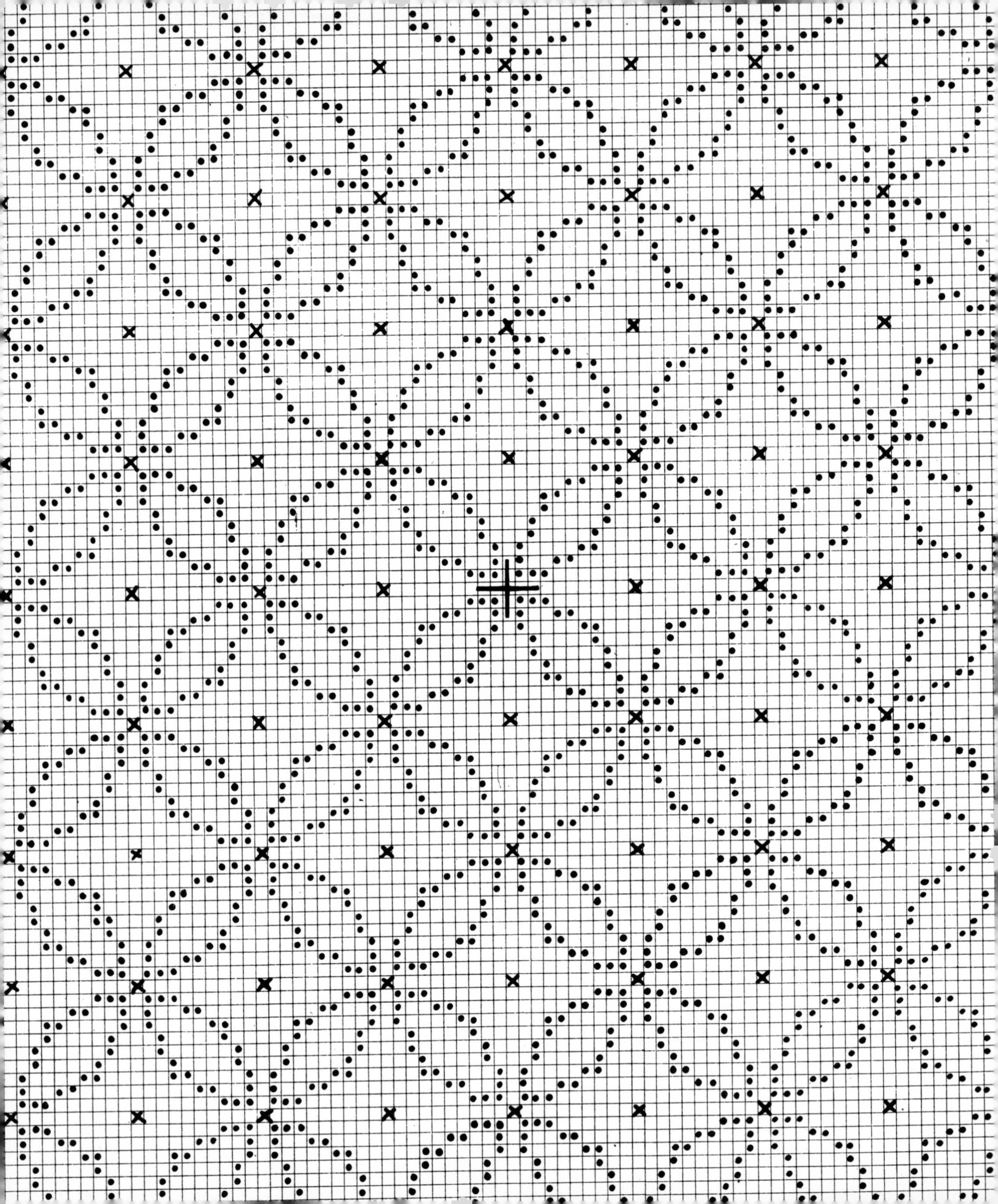

8. Pattern Sheet IV: The Circle

This pattern sheet adds the circle to our repertoire of shapes. More accurately the shape is one that looks very much like a circle but is really a sequence of stitches approximating a circle. This facsimile however works very well for our purposes. The network of intersecting circles (designated by the dotted arcs) allows us to create designs containing scallops, waves, and many other curved lines. Moreover, because the measurements of this pattern sheet coincide with those of pattern sheet II, we can add vertical, horizontal, and diagonal lines to the curved ones and produce an enormous variety of shapes.

Measuring, Marking, and Stitching

As with pattern sheets II and III, the linear structure is paramount; the unit measurements from **X** to **X** are therefore counted inclusively and the boundaries of the shapes are stitched first.

Each **X** on this pattern sheet is in the same position it was in on pattern sheet II. In the former case, the **X**'s designated the corners of the square; here, they designate the radii of the circles. Each circle has an **X** in the center and four **X**'s on its circumference. Since these **X**'s, like those of pattern sheet II, are 11 boxes apart counted inclusively, each circle has a radius of 11 boxes, from the center **X** to each **X** on its circumference. Thus 11 is both the horizontal and vertical measurement for this pattern sheet. This means that the center rules of the canvas will be divided into units of 11 threads counted inclusively, exactly like the center rules for pattern sheet II.

Fig. 158.   Part of pattern sheet IV.

On this pattern sheet we are concerned not with a diagonal going from one **X** to the next but with an arc. Since we cannot mark a curved line in an unbroken path on either the squares of the graph paper or the thread intersections of the canvas, we have a situation similar to that presented by the diagonals of the equilateral triangle. And there is a similar solution. Each arc is marked and stitched in a stepped sequence of fifteen stitches counted inclusively from one **X** to the next **X**. This sequence, only slightly more complicated than the one used for pattern sheet III, includes stitches that are grouped together vertically as well as stitches that are placed side by side, grouped horizontally.

The placement of the stitches is always the same: an arc that crests at either the top or bottom of the circle (C and D) always has three stitches placed horizontally next to the **X**, and an arc that crests at the side of the circle (A and B) always has three stitches placed vertically next to the **X**, (Fig. 159). Whether you work the vertical stitches or the horizontal stitches of the sequence first depends on the shape you are outlining, but if you start the sequence with the three vertical stitches you will always end it with the three horizontal stitches and vice versa. Basically the sequence, beginning and ending with one stitch at **X**, may be described as follows: one—three—two—two-and-one corner—two—three—one. It is marked and sewn on the thread intersections of the canvas along the same stepped path indicated by the dots. (Figs. 160 and 161).

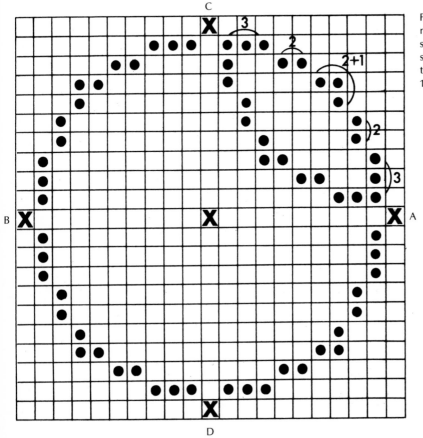

Fig. 159. The vertical and horizontal measurements of this pattern sheet are the same as pattern sheet II: 11 boxes from **X** to **X**, counted inclusively. Instead of diagonals, we have the arcs of the circle. Each arc is counted and worked in the 15-stitch sequence shown.

The stitch sequence is always worked from right to left, but it may be worked up or down the canvas. Thus, in working an entire circle, you would start at A (Fig. 159) and either work up the canvas to C and continue down to B, or work down the canvas to D and continue up to B. In both cases, it is then necessary to turn the canvas upside down and work the sequence from right to left again to complete the circle.

In working two arcs to form a leaf shape (Fig. 159), you again start at the right with stitch **X** and work one arc up the canvas to point C, then turn the canvas upside down to work the opposing arc. Since you will be using this fifteen-stitch sequence to work all curved lines, it is advisable to practice drawing and stitching the outline of a circle several times on a small piece of canvas. After repeating the sequence a few times, you will find that you have committed it to memory, a great aid to drawing and stitching these designs.

Fig. 160. The circle is marked on the thread intersections of the canvas according to the same sequence by which the boxes are counted.

Fig. 161. The outline forms a sewn boundary between adjacent shapes. The stitch sequence must be worked from right to left, but it may be worked up or down the canvas.

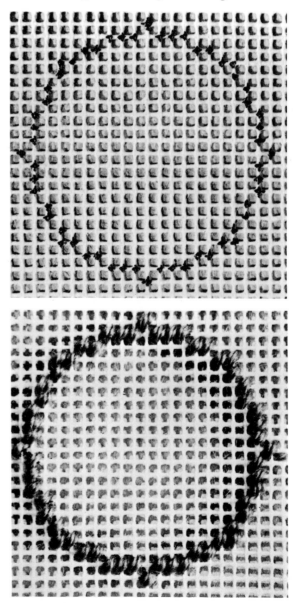

135

When enlarging the designs on tracing paper placed over the pattern sheet, treat the stepped sequence as a freely drawn curve. When transferring the design to the canvas, however, mark the curves as stepped lines *on* the thread intersections, as shown in Fig. 160.

The center rules are drawn and marked off *on* the threads of the canvas (Fig. 162), using the same horizontal and vertical count as pattern sheet II (11 threads from **X** to **X** counted inclusively). The maximum measurement of the total pattern sheet is 161 stitches horizontally and vertically.

Unlike the basic units of the previous pattern sheets, the circles, and the arcs that form them, cannot be enlarged. No circle can be larger or smaller than the size indicated on the pattern sheet (each diameter is 21 stitches) and no arc can extend more than one fifteen-stitch sequence without changing direction. Despite this, the opportunities for varying the designs are far from limited. Straight lines may be drawn from one **X** to another and be incorporated into the design. Since the **X**'s of this pattern sheet coincide with those of pattern sheet II, the straight and curved lines may also be combined to form entirely different shapes. In addition, a design based on this pattern sheet may be combined with one based on pattern sheet II to form a new design, such as the one in Fig. 105 (page 88). (Each radius on this pattern sheet is actually one side of the square unit in pattern sheet II, and each circle here can be inscribed in a large square formed by four of those basic units.)

When straight lines are added, they are of course marked as described in Chapter 6 and worked as described in Chapter 2. After all the outlines have been worked, the shapes are filled in with basket weave and single tent stitches in either the same or contrasting colors.

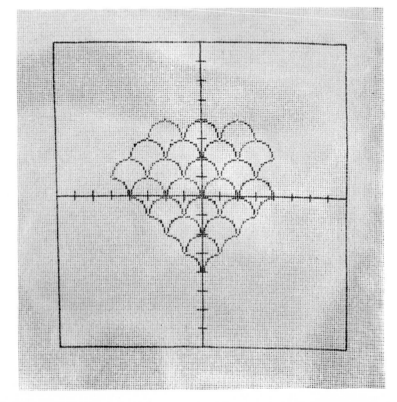

Fig. 162.   The center rules are drawn and marked off on the threads of the canvas according to the 11-thread count used for pattern sheet II.

Pattern IV-1

In this pattern, we take only those circles of the pattern sheet which do not overlap. The pattern is useful as a band or border, taking one row of circles, or simply the row of semi-circles which appear at the top and bottom.

If you wish to practice sewing the circle sequence, try making a sampler of this pattern, working the design 4 circles high by 4 circles wide. Make each circle a different color, upon a ground of a single color. Pick your favorite hues and work the outline of each circle with the yarn you will use to fill in the circle. Begin by outlining the circles and work from right to left. You will be surprised to see how attractive this simple design can become. You can also expand this idea and use the entire pattern for a pillow, coloring it in a similar manner.

IV-1

Fig. 163. This sewn detail shows the most basic pattern possible, that of the pattern sheet itself. Here, however, the outlines of overlapping circles have been included. This can be used to advantage as background patterning, with either the four-leaf clover shapes (on the left) or the scalloped diamond shapes (on the right) brought to the fore.

IV-2

Pattern IV-2

This design is based on the same principles as the preceding one, the only difference being that every other circle is omitted, both horizontally and vertically, and horizontal and vertical lines are included. The source of this pattern is a fourteenth-century Italian design of inlaid marble, which was colored to form a counterchange (as illustrated in Fig. 164). To maintain the visual balance shown, use an outline of a neutral color and fill in the shapes with any color you wish, but always retain the proper dark and light relationships.

This is a popular patchwork pattern, used with only slight variations and variously known as "Steeplechase," "Drunkard's Path," or "Mill Wheel."

Fig. 164.   Coloring for counterchange pattern.

Pattern IV-3

Segments of the circle give us this scale pattern, reminiscent of the scales of a fish or the way feathers grow on the neck of a bird. The pattern has been found in several different cultures at various times: on a column from the crypt of Canterbury Cathedral, Kent, England; on a sixteenth-century Venetian glass vase; on a sixteenth-century Turkish jug of painted, glazed earthenware; on a monument in a Renaissance Italian church. This universality is not surprising, since this is a basic pattern, easily adapted to many designs and uses.

In the example shown in color on page 158, each row of scallops is colored differently, using taste and preference alone as a guide. (Each scallop was outlined with the color with which it was filled in, starting at the bottom and working up.) This principle can be used for many of the patterns given, as well as this one. It works best with those designs that are most basic, having just one or two repeated elements which run in lines or rows.

IV-3

Pattern IV-4

This is a free interpretation of an Egyptian border pattern, which has been adapted for a belt (see color page 158). The pattern takes up 1½ units of the pattern sheet.

IV-4

IV-5

Pattern IV-5

This cloud-motif pattern, found in such diverse cultures as Japanese and Arabian, is obtained by omitting sections of the semicircles. In the work shown (Fig. 165), the cloud shapes are colored in a vertical stripe sequence, with the centers being constant. In this work also, each shape is outlined with its fill-in color, starting at the bottom and working up.

Fig. 165.   Design for the front piece of a handbag, by Susan Peimer, on No. 12 mesh with tapestry yarn. The needlepoint measures approximately 8½ by 10 inches, and is worked in red, blue, green, and yellow yarn.

Pattern IV-6

This line drawing is actually·four-in-one. In it, scalloped lines are crossed by straight lines in four different ways. You may easily extend any of the four to cover the pattern sheet.

IV-6

IV-7

Pattern IV-7

In this design, one of the patterns of the preceding line drawing is extended and made into a total design. Any of the remaining three could be treated in the same way.

The lower left-hand design of pattern IV-6 is used for the left side of this pattern, and is mirrored on the right. The meeting place in the center makes the shield-shapes that are emphasized in the sewn work. The worked canvas is shown made into an envelope purse, with the flap echoing the scalloped lines of the pattern (Fig. 166). The design is colored exactly the same under the flap as it is on it.

Fig. 166. Envelope bag designed by Winifred Bendiner and worked by Muriel Kahn on No. 10 mesh; the bag measures 12 by 10 inches. The outline is white, the same color as the two lightest shapes in the center of the design. (See color page 160.)

Pattern IV-8

The source of this pattern is a design painted on an apron, from Japan. Variations of it are also found in such diverse places as England (Iron-Age pottery) and Assyria (carved-stone capital). It can be seen as superimposed square shapes with blunted corners, or as concentric rings (as it is colored in the partly completed needlepoint in Fig. 167).

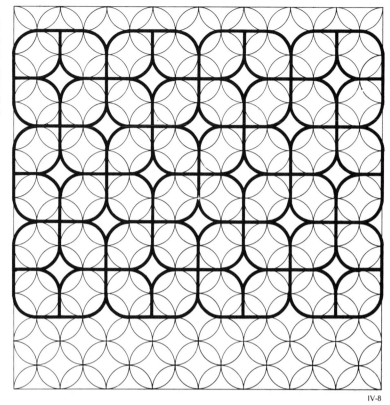

IV-8

Fig. 167. A portion of pattern IV-8 worked in five colors. The outline is the same color as the diamond-like shapes. The four light shapes grouped around the diamond at the top will become the center of the completed work.

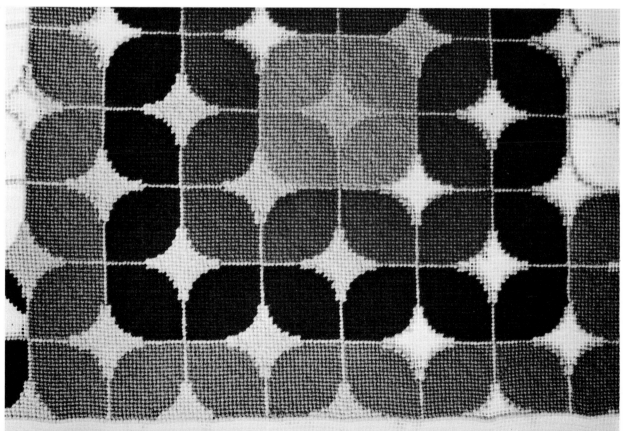

IV-9

Pattern IV-9

This pattern of S-curves makes a basic shape, often used historically, called the ogee. The ogee is to curvilinear designs what the hexagon or octagon is to straight-line designs: a second-rank basic figure. As such, it is used to construct the following four patterns (IV-10 through IV-13). It appears in various positions, and in combination with additional lines and shapes.

As a single shape the ogee is quite large and can be used as a decorative structure within which small figures (birds, flowers, etc.) may be placed, as in Fig. 168. In that piece, the flower was designed within the ogee by leaving the enlarged, traced drawing taped over the pattern sheet and marking the tracing paper to correspond with the appropriate graph boxes beneath. Follow the flower pattern as you would any charted embroidery design.

Fig. 168. A pattern of ogees enclosing flower forms. Patterns with large shapes such as this one lend themselves well to this use.

Pattern IV-10

Ogee shapes may be constructed running horizontally or vertically, or, as shown in this pattern, both horizontally and vertically at the same time. This design appears on an Indian cotton-printer's block of the nineteenth century. The same configuration, seen as a waved band pattern, was used by Oriental silk weavers for making many beautiful designs.

IV-10

IV-11

Pattern IV-11

This pattern again illustrates how different two very closely related patterns can look. This design is exactly the same as the preceding one, with the sole addition of straight lines which cut across the ogee shapes. It was used in Roman mosaic pavements and medieval wall paintings. The small drawing (Fig. 169) illustrates one way to color this design, namely, as a counterchange. When sewing this pattern, use a neutral color for outlining, to retain symmetry in the size of the shapes.

Fig. 169.   Coloring pattern as a counterchange.

Pattern IV-12

This pattern combines the ogee with the cloud-forms of pattern IV-5, producing the eight-sided figure that appears between the other shapes. These new figures are pleasing in their own right, and will serve particularly well as a background for free-form shapes (Fig. 170), or to enclose other designs, as in pattern IV-9.

IV-12

Fig. 170. Needlepoint pillow by Winifred Bendiner, measuring approximately 13½ by 10 inches, worked on No. 12 mesh. Free-form leaf shapes were superimposed over this large, curvilinear pattern. (See color page 161.)

IV-13

Pattern IV-13

This pattern is an original one and it simply combines two very basic designs: the pattern sheet itself, and the ogee pattern (pattern IV-10). Three ogees appear horizontally, and two ogees appear vertically. The points of the four outer ogee shapes are connected by straight 45° diagonal lines, creating a diamond-shaped frame around the center motif. In the example (Fig. 171), each ogee and each leaf shape is filled in with the same color with which it is outlined.

If this design is to be made into a pillow, it is advisable to extend the background approximately one inch on all four sides, so that the center motif will not curve around the edges of the pillow when it is stuffed (this does not include the four extra rows ordinarily worked around the perimeter when making a pillow).

Fig. 171. Needlepoint pattern designed by Howard Kalish and worked by Anita Gregory, on No. 10 mesh with Persian yarn. The center ogee is white and is surrounded by green leaf shapes on a yellow background; the other ogee shapes are ochre. The outer background is outlined in orange and filled in with orange and brown.

Pattern IV-14

This pattern, which has been gleaned from Aegean and Egyptian sources (the wall of a tomb at Thebes; Egyptian painted ceiling, Eighteenth Dynasty), is also often found in Oriental art. It shows how circles connected by tangent lines may make a starlike form. In the sewn detail (Fig. 172), the design is cropped and colored in such a way as to emphasize the circles. This shows how a pattern may be visually transformed, without changing it, simply by emphasizing one aspect and playing down another.

Another transformation is shown in the full-size pillow design (Fig. 173). Here the star shapes are brought to the fore, and the circles are concealed by making them the same color as the background. The star shapes are outlined in the color with which they are to be filled in. The small squares are placed on the intersections of the diagonal lines of pattern sheet II. Each small square is made up of nine stitches (3 by 3).

IV-14

Fig. 172. A small design with five circles, in two shades of orange on a yellow background. The outline is the same color as the circles.

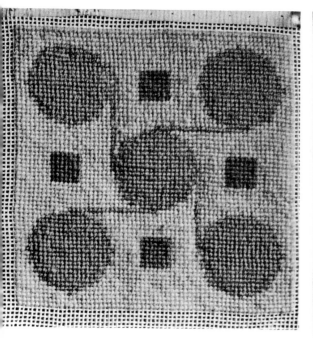

Fig. 173. Pillow design emphasizes the star shapes. (See color page 160.)

IV-15

IV-16

Pattern IV-15

This is a variation on an Egyptian design. The small squares are each 3 stitches by 3 stitches.

Pattern IV-16

This pattern is also a variation on an Egyptian design. It would be especially suitable to be worked on No. 14 mesh, extending the given design, and thus including more of the large enclosed shapes. The four-petaled flowers are examples of how a smaller shape can be used within a larger one. Outline the design in a different color than any used to fill in the large shapes, preferably a neutral tone. This is to maintain visual balance. The small squares in the design are each 3 by 3 stitches.

Pattern IV-17

This original design is a variation on the appearance of sculpted rope-molding of the Renaissance and Middle Ages. As you can see in the line drawing, this design forms a diamond-shaped area on the canvas. The background can be worked in a corresponding diamond shape around the design and the finished canvas can be viewed as a diamond (Fig. 174), or it can be turned on its side and viewed as a square.

IV-17

Fig. 174. Needlepoint designed by Winifred Bendiner and worked by Mae Eisenberg; it measures approximately 14 inches square on No. 12 mesh. The background was extended one unit on each side of the diamond shape. (See color page 163.)

151

IV-18

Pattern IV-18

This pattern and the piece of work which accompanies it (Fig. 175) show how a design may be extended to fit a particular size. In this case, a band pattern (line drawing) is repeated side-to-side to fit the dimensions of a piano bench.

In the sewn work, each of the scalloped wing-shapes is outlined in the color with which it is to be filled in, starting at the bottom. The diamond shapes remain after outlining, and are filled in with another color.

Fig. 175. Cushion for a piano bench by Yetta Ostrow. It measures 32 by 14 inches, is worked on No. 10 mesh with Persian yarn. (See color page 163.)

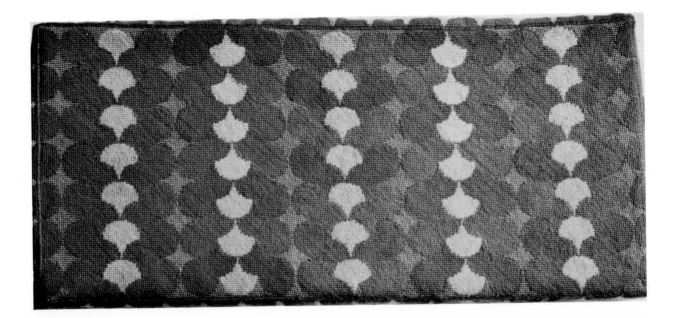

Pattern IV-19

I have spoken of juxtaposing two patterns, with one serving as the figure and the other as the background. This pattern is a good example. Since pattern sheets II and IV fit together, IV-19 was expressly created as an emblem motif to be placed on a background taken from pattern II-13 (slightly modified to combine with the central design). The results are shown on pages 88 and 157.

To juxtapose these two designs, first trace the center motif on a large piece of tracing paper over pattern sheet IV. Then place the tracing paper over pattern sheet II to draw the background.

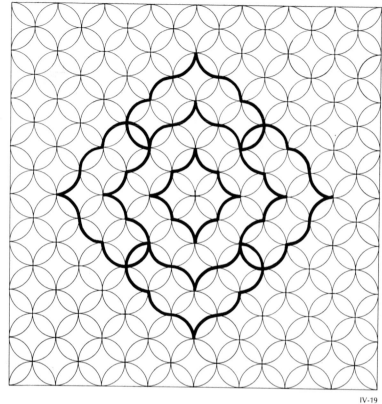

IV-19

IV-20

Pattern IV-20

This is an imaginative design freely drawn on the lines of the pattern sheet. Squares and diamonds, more clearly expressed on pattern sheet II, are used in combination with the curved shapes of pattern sheet IV. The design is given two units larger on two sides than the pattern sheet. To make a smaller needlepoint, work on No. 12 or No. 14 canvas. In the needlepoint shown in Fig. 176, the central motif and the rectangular border are worked with darker yarn, while the scalloped rows, center ovals, and the small dots are primarily light tones.

Fig. 176. Needlepoint designed by Winifred Bendiner and worked by Nancy Migdal, in shades of red and beige. The outline within the design is overstitched with gold thread.

Pattern IV-21

This motif and the border in Fig. 177, taken together, make the needlepoint design shown in color on page 160, a needlepoint which spans two cultures and two pattern sheets. The central motif is freely based upon Islamic forms and is drawn on pattern sheet IV; the border design hails from the Middle Ages, and is drawn on pattern sheet II.

When tracing the design, first draw the border on pattern sheet II. The remaining shape in the center will be 10 by 10 units square, an area equal in size to the central design of "trees, mountains and stars." In the border, the sewn outline will always remain visible, while the outlines in the center design are always worked in the same colors as the shapes themselves. In the center design, single light-colored stitches are randomly placed to create the effect of a starry sky.

IV-21

Fig. 177. Border pattern based on pattern sheet II.

IV-22

IV-22a

Pattern IV-22

This pattern is derived from a decorative border which forms a frame around a church fresco, painted by a contemporary of Giotto, in Assisi, Italy. The two drawings are the patterns for the front (b) and the back-and-flap piece (a) of the shoulder bag shown in Fig. 178 (also see color page 157). To produce the effect of equal-size shapes without an outline, the rows of parallelograms are marked and sewn as in pattern sheet I. The bag's sides and shoulder strap are formed from a one-inch wide band of parallelograms. The center, cloverleaf shapes are outlined in the background color and the semicircles at either side are then outlined in the color with which they will be filled in.

Fig. 178. Shoulder bag designed by Susan Schoenfeld and worked by Lillian Schoenfeld. The bag measures approximately 12 inches square, and is worked on No. 10 mesh with tapestry yarn. For instructions on how to assemble a shoulder bag, see page 168.

IV-22b

Color Plate 1. Needlepoint, using various tones of gray to color pattern III-18, was made into a handbag by Susan Schoenfeld.

Color Plate 3. Here light shades of the primary colors (red, yellow, and blue) and of the secondary colors (purple, orange, and green) create a pastel effect. Red, purple, and green are rotated around the hexagons in one horizontal row; and yellow, blue, and orange are rotated around the hexagons of an alternate row. (See pattern III-14.)

Color Plate 2. The contrast between the subdued background tone and the intense colors of the bands of parallelograms contributes much to the striking appearance of this shoulder bag. (See pattern IV-22.)

Color Plate 4. This bench cover is worked on No. 10 mesh with three shades of pink, three shades of purple, a pale blue-green, gray-green, and gray. The outline is the same dark purple as the small diamond shapes. The center motif is pattern IV-19 and it is surrounded by pattern II-13, whose shapes merge with the motif in the center.

Color Plate 5. In this exciting piece by Nancy and Howard Kalish, yellow serves as a light background for the flashing primary and secondary colors. (See pattern I-16.)

Color Plate 6. Hexagon box pillow worked in light to dark tones of the primary colors. The outline throughout is the same gray color as the hexagon in the center. (See pattern III-20.)

Color Plate 7. An arrangement of the needlepoint pillows shown for patterns I-13 and I-15. The coloring in the bottom pillow follows the Egyptian original.

Color Plate 8. This elegant needlepoint and velvet pillow by Winifred Bendiner shows what can be done with a simple pattern by experimenting with unusual color combinations. Twenty-two colors are used to fill in the rows of scallop shapes. Needlepoint, worked on No. 12 mesh with tapestry yarn, measures 9 by 18½ inches. (See pattern IV-3.)

Color Plate 9. A brightly colored pillow made to go in a baby's room, by Susan Schoenfeld. It is approximately 12 inches square, worked on No. 10 mesh with tapestry yarn. The entire design is outlined with red yarn. (See pattern III-23.)

Color Plate 10. Needlepoint belt based on pattern IV-4, by Elinor Migdal; worked on No. 12 mesh, making it 2½ inches wide. It is finished with mitred corners and is lined with satin ribbon.

Color Plate 11. Patchwork quilt by Jeffrey Gutcheon. Diagonal lines of quilting and solid rectangular borders repeat and accentuate the lines of this design. (See patchwork pattern 9.)

Color Plate 12. Needlepoint pillow by Susan Schoenfeld; worked on No. 10 mesh with tapestry yarn and based on pattern II-9. The single white stitches placed within the cross shapes accent the design.

Color Plate 13. Needlepoint belt by Nancy Migdal. Pattern I-8 is extended horizontally; the shapes were made smaller by halving all the lines in the design. The belt, approximately 1¾ inches wide, is worked on No. 12 mono-mesh with two strands of Persian yarn. It is lined with a decorative red, white, and blue ribbon.

Color Plate 14. Baby's coverlet based on pattern III-2 ("Baby's Blocks"), by Winifred Bendiner. Each side of the diamond shapes measures 2 units, just as it is given in the drawn pattern.

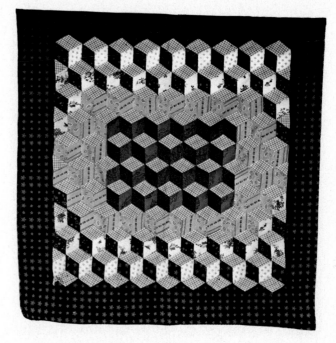

Color Plate 15. In this coverlet, three floral prints are tastefully combined with green and white. (See patchwork pattern 8.)

Color Plate 16. This design by Winifred Bendiner was worked by Netty Cohen and is based on pattern IV-14. The circular shapes of the pattern are completely hidden by working them in the same color as the outline.

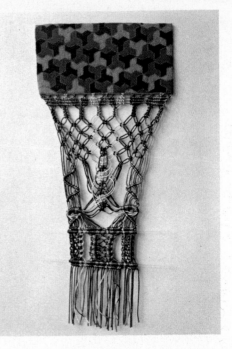

Color Plate 17. Needlepoint and macramé hanging by Joanne Leeds; pattern III-11 worked on No. 14 mesh with two strands of Persian yarn. The macramé cords are mounted before they are knotted by first turning back the edges of unworked mesh and then running the cords through the doubled-over threads of the canvas.

Color Plate 18. This scale pattern of cool blues and grays makes an abstract design reminiscent of the sea and seashells. When it is made into an envelope bag, the scalloped edges of the shapes form an appropriate flap. (See pattern IV-7.)

Color Plate 19. The fact that this design, by Howard Kalish, reads as a picture in a frame makes it ideal for a wall hanging. The central motif was created from pattern sheet IV and the border from pattern sheet II. The shaded, three-dimensional effect of the border was created by working three rows of the dark tone (red or blue), two rows of the light-middle tone (pink or light blue), one row of the same dark tone, and three rows of ecru, within the shapes bounded by the black outlines. (See pattern IV-21.)

Color Plate 20. Color combinations are most important in this needlepoint pillow worked by Mollie Heller. This design alternates rows of light and dark octagons with accenting squares in a gray-yellow and two shades of yellow. The outlines are in both dark and bright green.

Color Plate 21. The needlepoint pillow on the left is based on pattern III-5; the one on the right is based on pattern III-6. The patchwork pillow by Winifred Bendiner is based on the same pattern sheet and the hexagon shapes are the same size as the larger ones in the needlepoints. They are made of printed silk from old ties, and the patchwork is applied to a velvet background.

Color Plate 22. This design by Winifred Bendiner is an example of an adjacent color arrangement. It is based upon the natural green color of the leaf forms, and goes subtly towards blue-green and blue. (See pattern IV-12.)

Color Plate 23. Needlepoint design by Yetta Kalish. A border effect is created within this patchwork-like design by working the shapes along the perimeter in shades of blue, gray, and gold. Blue squares accent the corners of the design. (See pattern II-24.)

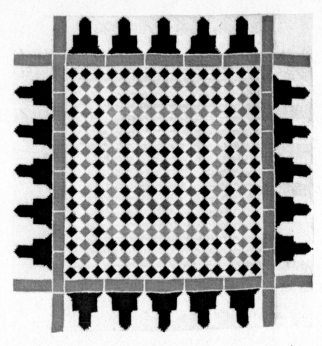

Color Plate 25. Strong contrasting colors heighten the graphic effect of this design. The border is simply the lines of the pattern sheet filled in with four colors in such a way that each small triangle is directly opposite one of the same color. (See pattern III-21.)

Color Plate 24. In this piece by Pat Price, the colors of the yarn were chosen to closely approximate the ceramic tile wall in the Alhambra, from which this design was adapted (pattern II-1). The colored diamond rows are interposed with white ones and the entire pattern is outlined with white yarn.

Color Plate 26. Needlepoint pillow by Betty Brean. Different feelings can be expressed, and different effects achieved, with the same pattern, through the use of color and tone. Compare this piece with the one shown in plate 28; both are based on pattern II-11. Here, strong contrasts create a bold design. The border is a double row of semi-circles, with each row outlined in its darkest color. The entire pillow is 16 inches square.

Color Plate 27. Needlepoint by Susanna Briselli. Colors close to those of the original Spanish tiles were chosen to make this stately design (pattern II-12). The entire pattern is outlined in ecru yarn, and filled in with ecru, yellow, blue, reddish-brown, and royal blue.

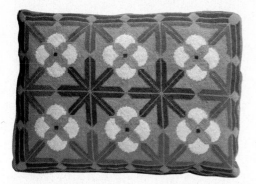

Color Plate 28. A harmonious color combination has been created in this handsome needlepoint pillow by Netty Barash. The entire pattern outline is stitched with orange yarn, the dominant color of the piece. Four additional colors are used: dark burgundy, rose, gold, and peach. (See pattern II-11.)

Color Plate 30. Colors of the yarn were carefully chosen to simulate the effect of transparent panes of glass, creating darker areas where they overlap. (See pattern III-19.)

Color Plate 29. The "ropelike" forms alternate a bright and a dull orange (the latter is subtly different in the inner configuration than in the outer one). (See pattern IV-17.)

Color Plate 31. The pattern on the side of this cushion is a variation of the design on the top (pattern IV-18), with scallop shapes placed side by side. The sides are 2 inches wide and are attached to the front and back pieces with overcast stitches in much the same way as the pieces for a shoulder bag are assembled.

Color Plate 32. In this cheerful patchwork by Marcia Schonzeit, gaily colored prints are combined with bright, solid colors. The square blocks are separated by strips of black. (See patchwork pattern 1.)

Color Plate 34. Patchwork quilt with an embroidered center, based on pattern sheet I, by Donna Gould. This large quilt was made by piecing together 7-by-7-inch blocks. Each block is made up of: four 2-by-2-inch squares, one 3-by-3-inch square, and four 2-by-3-inch rectangles.

Color Plate 33. Pattern II-20 worked in needlepoint, and the same pattern enlarged for patchwork (pattern 2). The same basic, linear pattern can create an entirely different design when worked in different colors, sizes, and materials.

Color Plate 35. Needlepoint pillow by Winifred Bendiner, on No. 12 mesh, and patchwork by Marcia Schonzeit, both made from the "Baby's Blocks" (pattern III-2). The size of the diamond shapes in the needlepoint is as given in the pattern; for the patchwork each line of the diamond was increased to 3 units.

9. Finishing Your Needlepoint

Blocking

Since the canvas is usually pulled out of its original shape when the stitches are worked, the finished piece should be blocked to make it reassume that shape. (Blocking can also smooth out unevenness in the stitches.) The basket weave tends to distort the shape of the canvas less than any other stitch, but the work should still be blocked.

First, draw the intended shape and size of the finished canvas on a piece of paper. (If the work is on No. 10 canvas and it is within the dimensions of the pattern sheet, the shape can be traced directly from the sheet.) Tape this piece of paper to a flat board. The board can be either a piece of softwood or Homosote gotten at a lumberyard.

Lay the work face down on the paper. Placing push-pins through the canvas in the unworked margin around the needlepoint area, pin two top corners of the canvas into proper shape. Then, with a sponge and water, dampen the back of the finished piece of work. You may wet the piece quite a bit; as long as the medium you have used for marking the pattern on the canvas is waterproof, the water won't damage it. I have found that if the piece is steamed with an iron rather than fully dampened with water, the needlepoint will remain out of shape when removed from the board. Once the work is wet, however, it becomes pliable and can be made to conform to the shape of the traced outline.

Ease the dampened piece into shape, and pin the other two corners of the canvas. Then pin at one-inch intervals along all four sides, keeping the pins about one inch away from the sewn area. Blocking is best accomplished by keeping an even tension while pinning the work. Do not complete one side all at once. After you have positioned the corners, pin the center of each side and continue outward from the centers to the corners, alternately working on opposite sides of the piece until you have finished. Allow the work to remain pinned to the board until it is completely dry. This may take as long as three days, depending on the humidity in the air.

Making a Pillow

Almost all the patterns given in this book are designed within the framework of a 16-inch square. This makes them directly suitable for use as pillow patterns. Therefore, I will focus here on the simplest and most direct way to complete such a project.

After the work is removed from the blocking board, trim the unworked canvas margin to within ½ inch of the worked area. Cut a piece of fabric (I prefer velvet or corduroy) the same size as the outer dimensions of the trimmed canvas (including the ½ inch of unworked mesh). Placing the right sides of the fabric and needlepoint together, pin and baste these two layers along the three sides of the square form. Then, stitch them together either by machine or by hand, placing the line of stitches between the last row of the design and the extra rows you have added at each edge for that purpose. If you are not using penelope or locked mesh, you may also want to sew the raw edges of the canvas around the perimeter with a large machine stitch, to keep them from unraveling.

Clip the fabric and canvas at the two sewn corners and press the seams open. (You may trim the canvas further if it seems too bulky.) Turn this envelope of material right side out and insert a ready-made pillow, or one you have made yourself, which is about one inch larger in its outside dimensions than the envelope is. For example, if your envelope is 16 by 16 inches, the inside pillow should be at least 17 by 17 inches. You may consider using an even larger pillow if you wish the finished piece to be firm rather than soft. Arrange the stuffing so that it fills out the corners of your work.

Once the pillow is inside, turn in the open edges of the canvas and the fabric and sew them together, using a small overcast stitch. If the needlepoint requires cleaning at a later date, simply rub the surface with a small piece of rough cloth dampened with cleaning fluid; then rub it with a dry cloth. If you wish to remove the needlepoint casing for cleaning, open the overcast side; resew it when you have cleaned it and have reinserted the inside pillow.

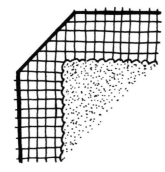

Mitred Corners

When using your needlepoint for a flat object, such as a wall hanging, belt, or handbag, you should make mitred corners on the back of the work. Place the work wrong side up. Crop the unworked canvas to about ½ inch from the needlepoint area at each side and at each corner (Fig. 179). On unlocked canvas you should then run a line of glue along the cut edges to prevent unraveling. Next, fold a corner of the unworked canvas down over the worked area at the same 45° angle at which it is cut (Fig. 180). Then fold the canvas margin on each adjacent side over the corner (Fig. 181). Sew the two diagonal edges together with a whipstitch (Fig. 182). Press the work flat.

Fig. 179. Trim the unworked canvas along each side and at a 45° angle on each corner. (Heavy lines show cut edges of canvas.)

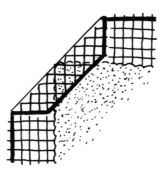

Fig. 180. Fold the corner over so it covers the back of the needlepoint.

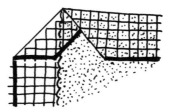

Fig. 181. Fold one side over the covered corner.

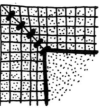

Fig. 182. Fold the adjacent side over the same corner and sew the two diagonal edges together with a whipstitch.

Assembling a Three-Piece Shoulder Bag

First you need to work three pieces of canvas: a square or rectangular piece for the front of the bag; a long rectangular piece for the back and the front flap; and a long narrow strip for the sides and shoulder strap (Fig. 183). The piece for the back should correspond in width to the piece for the front and should be long enough so the upper part may be folded over the front piece to make an adequate flap. The flap should cover at least one-third of the bag front. The third piece of canvas, the narrow strip, should be long enough to fit around the bottom and two sides of the square or rectangular front while looping around the top to form the shoulder strap (Fig. 184).

When the design has been completed on each piece of canvas, sew an extra row of stitches around the perimeter of each piece. Work the stitches around the perimeter of the narrow strip so that they slant in the *opposite* direction from that of the stitches worked within the design area. This will make the stitching of the two larger pieces to the strip easier.

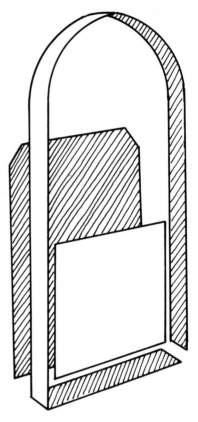

Fig. 184.   How the three pieces fit together.

Fig. 183.   Three pieces of canvas worked by Nancy Migdal, in Persian yarn on No. 10 mesh, to be made into a shoulder bag. The 12-inch square (the front of the bag) and the 21-by-12 inch rectangle (the back and flap) are based on pattern II-10. The continuous checkered strip is 65 inches by 1½ inches and will become the bottom, sides, and strap.

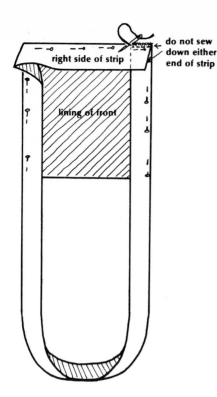

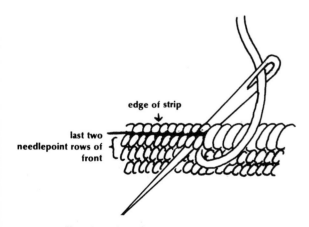

Block the work and finish each piece with mitred corners. Press the edges gently on the wrong side. Line each canvas piece separately with a piece of suitable fabric (silk or cotton). Cut the lining ⅜ of an inch larger all around for each canvas piece. Turn under and baste this ⅜-inch margin along each edge of each lining. Then pin and baste the lining pieces to the needlepoint pieces with the wrong sides of the fabrics together. Sew them together with a small overcast stitch. Remove the basting and press the lining lightly, being careful not to flatten the needlepoint stitches. If you wish the bag to have more body, insert a piece of stiff interlining between the needlepoint and the lining, and tack it in place to keep it from slipping.

Assemble the lined pieces of the bag by first attaching the strip to the front piece, beginning at the corner indicated (Fig. 185). Place the lined sides of the pieces together and pin or hold the strip in place. Then sew the edges of the work with an even overcast stitch, inserting the needle between the last two rows of needlepoint stitches on both pieces (Fig. 186). Sew the strip to the front piece along three sides, using the same color yarn as the principle design color.

Pin the edges of the back-and-flap piece to the other edge of the strip and sew them together in the same way (Fig. 187). Begin and end the yarn through the overcast stitches on the wrong side of the work; once the bag is partially assembled this is most easily done by turning the work inside out. Where the bottom ends of the strip meet, stitch them together with the same overcast stitch.

Fig. 185. Sew the strip to the front piece, lined sides together.

Fig. 186. Sew the two edges together with overcast stitches.

Fig. 187. Pin or hold the back-and-flap piece to the strip and sew them together.

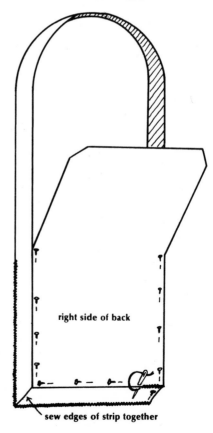

Fig. 188. Printed toile and polychrome chintz quilt. An historical example, courtesy of the Brooklyn Museum. The pinwheel motif is worked in different sizes.

10. Patchwork & Appliqué

Patchwork and appliqué are both needlecrafts which create decorative designs from small pieces of fabric cut into separate shapes. The shapes are either sewn together for patchwork or sewn to a larger fabric backing for appliqué. Both techniques have a long and rather well-documented history in Europe and Asia, and both flourished particularly when brought to these shores. For pioneer folk, every scrap of fabric had to be put to some use. "Waste not, want not" was a code of survival. In patchwork, this code was raised to the level of an art. Many beautiful, decorative designs were created by piecing together scraps left over from newly made garments, or the good parts of worn-out clothing, to make a large piece of fabric that could be fashioned into quilts and other useful articles.

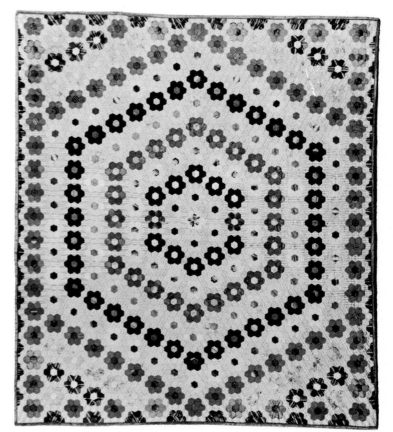

Fig. 189. Early nineteenth-century American patchwork quilt. (The Metropolitan Museum of Art, Bequest of Carolyn Fiske MacGregor, 1953; in memory of Caroline Brooks Gould.)

Patchwork, as distinct from appliqué, is the art of sewing the small pieces of fabric *to each other*, combining different prints and colors as desired. The beauty of a patchwork depends as much on a tasteful selection and combination of materials, prints, and colors as it does on the basic pattern. The results can be conceived of as a mosaic using fabric rather than tiles. (Indeed many patchwork patterns are derived from old mosaic or parquet designs.) The elements fit together like the pieces of a puzzle, with no loose ends or leftover pieces (Fig. 190). Therefore, geometric designs, which allow this kind of neat division and systematic reassembly, are especially appropriate.

In appliqué, the small pieces of fabric are sewn to the surface of a larger piece of material. (The word comes from the French *appliquer*, "to put, or lay, on.") Fine examples of appliqué have survived from the European Middle Ages, from Asia, and from Africa, as well as from here in America. Whereas patchwork has a functional *raison d'être*, allowing one to make a large piece of material from small bits and pieces, appliqué is purely decorative. The small pieces of fabric do not increase the size or the strength of the larger fabric to which they are applied, but they do enhance its beauty; they can make a large, dull piece of material into a delightfully decorative fabric.

Fig. 190. The fabric shapes of a patchwork fit together perfectly, like mosaic tile.

Using Designs Based on the Pattern Sheets

For both patchwork and appliqué one must cut out the shapes of the design. In many of the designs given for needlepoint, the shapes are smaller than you will wish them to be for patchwork or appliqué. Therefore, you will wish to enlarge the design elements to a suitable size. The pattern sheets make enlarging the shapes in a design especially easy. Fig. 191 shows how to enlarge a single shape by extending each of its lines the same multiple of basic units. All designs based on pattern sheets I, II and III can be enlarged in this way. Circle designs based on pattern sheet IV cannot be enlarged in the same way, but most shapes in those designs are large enough to be worked as given (Fig. 192).

How large you will want to make the shapes in a given design will depend on the object you intend to use it for—a large quilt, or a coverlet, a wall hanging, etc. You can determine to what extent a design should be enlarged by making an enlargement on tracing paper placed over the appropriate pattern sheet, and drawing enough of a repeat to include all the shapes in the design. This tracing can then be placed in its setting-to-be—for instance, on the bed where a quilt is to go—to see approximately how many shapes you will need, and whether they are too big or too small for the total design you have in mind.

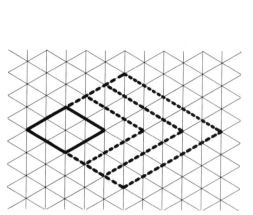

Fig. 191. A shape can be enlarged for patchwork by extending each of its lines an equal number of units on the pattern sheet.

Fig. 192. Late nineteenth-century American patchwork. Although the circular configurations here were achieved in a different way, they resemble those of pattern sheet IV and are the same size. Thus you can see that, while the circular designs given in this book cannot be enlarged, they are suitable for patchwork without enlargement. (The Metropolitan Museum of Art, Gift of Mrs. Russell Sage, 1916.)

For example, my mother was struck by pattern II-15 (page 90) and wanted to make a patchwork quilt from it. The shapes were much too small to work, so she multiplied them by three. Fig. 193 shows the center portion of pattern II-15 with all the elements multiplied by three: lines which were 1 unit long are now 3 units long; lines ½ a unit long become 1½ units long. This size was ideal for the quilt she wanted.

Once you have enlarged one shape in a design, all other shapes follow easily, almost automatically. The tracing will be a guide for cutting the fabric shapes to the proper size.

Fig. 193. A portion of pattern II-15 with all the elements three times the original size.

Fig. 194. Patchwork in progress by Lillian Schoenfeld. The fabric shapes are cut and pieced together for pattern II-15. Two printed and two solid-color fabrics create the light-dark coloration.

As patchwork depends on fitting pieces of fabric together, the shapes that work best—because of the economy with which they can be cut and assembled, and the strength they will have when sewn together—are simple shapes without notches or overhangs (Fig. 195). Shapes that do not fit into this category should first be separated into more basic shapes so the elements can more easily be pieced together when the fabric is cut and sewn. Fig. 196 shows three examples of notched shapes, with dotted lines indicating how the fabric should be cut into separate elements and pieced together.

Some designs have shapes that are too intricate or varied to be easily pieced. These are better worked in appliqué (see Fig. 207), or in a combination of patchwork and appliqué.

Fig. 195. Simple shapes can easily be cut in one piece and sewn to other shapes.

Fig. 196. More complicated shapes should first be cut into more basic ones and pieced together as a unit.

175

Patchwork Techniques

Each shape in a patchwork is drawn, cut, and formed with two templates, one the actual size of the shape and the other slightly larger. The actual-size template is used for making paper pattern-pieces; the larger template is for cutting the fabric. Starting with the design drawn actual size on tracing paper laid over the appropriate pattern sheet, the following steps describe how to make a hand-sewn patchwork.

First, put aside your preliminary tracing and place another sheet of fairly heavy tracing paper on the pattern sheet. Referring to the first tracing for measurements, draw each separate shape in the design as accurately as possible on the new tracing paper, using a ruler and a sharp pencil. Then cut out each shape very carefully on the drawn lines to obtain an actual-size template of each one. If a sturdier template is desired, you may place each of these shapes on a piece of cardboard, trace around it with pencil, and cut out an actual-size template of cardboard.

Each of the actual-size templates is now used for cutting paper pattern-pieces for each shape. You will need a separate pattern-piece for each piece of fabric to be used in the design; if one shape recurs eight times in the design, you will need eight paper pattern-pieces for that shape; if another shape recurs twelve times, you will need twelve pattern pieces for it, etc. Use ordinary lightweight paper. Place the template on top. Trace carefully around the edges of the template; then cut out the shape. Repeat this process until you have the correct number of pattern-pieces for each shape. Then put the pattern-pieces aside for the time being. Clip identical shapes together, to keep them in order.

The next step is to make a cardboard template of each shape, to be used for cutting the fabric. These templates should be larger to allow the edges of the fabric shapes to be turned under for sewing. Taking the actual-size template for a shape in the design, place it on a piece of stiff paper, such as oaktag, shirt cardboard, or fine sandpaper (which has the advantage of not slipping on the fabric). Mark the shape on the cardboard approximately ⅜ of an inch larger all around and cut it out (Fig. 197). Repeat this for each shape.

Fig. 197. The paper template is the same size as the shape in the design. The cardboard template beneath it is ⅜ of an inch larger all around.

Fig. 198.   The cardboard template is placed on the fabric and outlined so the shape may be cut.

Fig. 199.   One of the paper pattern-pieces is pinned to each piece of fabric.

Now use these cardboard templates to mark the fabric to be cut (Fig. 198). On light fabric, mark with pencil; on dark fabric, you may use tailor's chalk or light-colored pencil. (Sometimes a single shape in a design will have a right and a left side, like the parallelogram in Fig. 193; when cutting the fabric, simply flip the template over, and you will be able to cut pieces which face in both directions.) Cut as many fabric pieces as you will need for each shape in the design.

When everything has been cut out, take one fabric piece and a corresponding paper pattern-piece. Center the paper on the wrong side of fabric and pin securely (Fig. 199). Starting at one side of the shape, fold the fabric over the paper and baste the fold in place with large stitches through the paper and fabric. Continue along the peri-meter of the shape, folding the corners as indicated in Figs. 200 through 204, until all sides of the fabric are basted down.

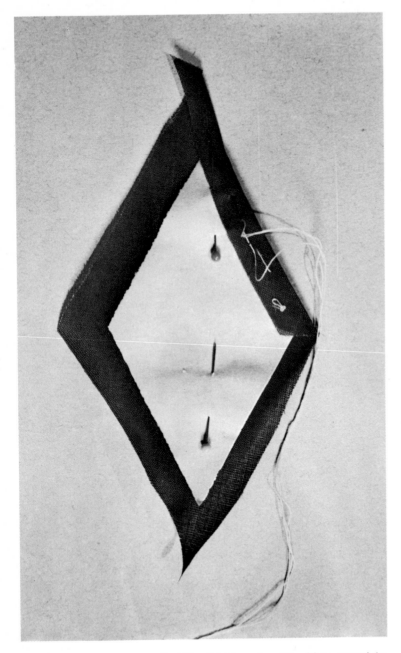

Fig. 200.   Fold the edge of the fabric around the paper pattern-piece and baste through both.

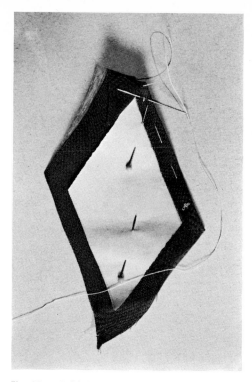

Fig. 201. Fold the material at the corner.

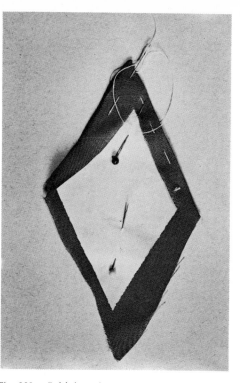

Fig. 202. Fold the edge over the paper and continue basting.

Fig. 203. Continue along the perimeter of the shape.

Fig. 204. The paper pattern is completely enclosed by the material.

179

Prepare enough shapes in this way so that you can begin to assemble the design. To sew two fabric pieces together, hold them with the right sides together and the edges to be sewn matching. Pin if desired, and sew the coinciding edges with a small overcasting stitch (Fig. 205). Knot at the end.

Each patchwork design has its own characteristics, which determine the order of assembly. In this case, the diamond-shaped fabric pieces are first sewn into hexagons, which are then pieced together to form pattern III-2 (page 110). The completed work is shown in color on page 164. Many of the designs based on pattern sheet III follow this principle, the fabric pieces being sewn into larger hexagons, diamonds, or triangles, which are then assembled to make the total piece. Other designs, like many traditional patchwork patterns, can be arranged into square blocks, or long strips, that can later be sewn together. Some designs simply start with a single shape to which another is added, and then another, like a growing ball of string, until the desired dimensions are achieved.

After a group of shapes has been sewn together, press the material on the wrong side to flatten it. It is easier to press each group separately than to iron the entire patchwork, and flattening the groups makes them fit together better.

Once your design is completely assembled and pressed, you may cut all the basting threads, pull them out, and remove the paper pattern-pieces.

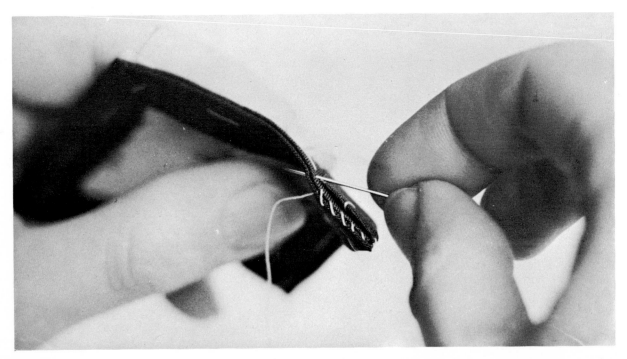

Fig. 205. Sew two completed shapes together with small overcasting stitches; hold the shapes with the right sides of the fabric pieces together.

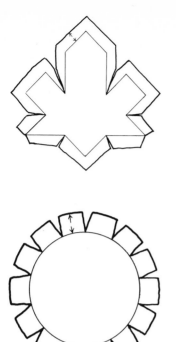

Appliqué Techniques

Any shape may be cut from fabric and sewn to the surface of another piece of fabric. Shapes may be applied to a large piece of fabric, or to smaller pieces, like squares or hexagons, which may then be sewn together to make a larger piece.

As in patchwork, you will need an enlarged tracing of the design and two templates for each shape: one actual size, and another ⅜ of an inch larger all around for cutting the fabric. The edges of the fabric pieces will have to be turned under to make a clean edge, except when you use a fabric such as felt, which does not fray when cut. (In that case, you need only the actual-size templates.)

Using the larger, cardboard templates, cut as many fabric pieces for each shape as you will need for your entire design. On each cut piece, on the right side of the fabric, center the smaller, paper template for that shape and carefully trace around it, using a sharpened pencil (light or dark colored, depending on the fabric).

Fold each side of the fabric shape along the marked outline, turning the edges of the material under to the wrong side, and baste the folds in place. This is the same procedure as the one described on page 178, except that there is no paper pattern-piece placed within the shape. Don't knot the basting thread. For more complicated shapes, it will be necessary to clip corners and curves before basting (Fig. 206). Press each basted shape on the wrong side.

Transfer the traced design to the foundation fabric (using one of the techniques that will be described in the following paragraph) to indicate exactly where each fabric piece goes. Pin or baste each fabric piece into place (Fig. 207) and sew it to the foundation fabric with a blind hemming stitch or a decorative embroidery stitch. Shapes such as those in Fig. 206 may fray slightly where they are clipped; this can be corrected by tucking the loose threads under the shape with the point of the needle as you stitch it into place.

Fig. 206. No paper insert is used for appliqué; the ⅜ of an inch margin shown by the arrows is drawn on the fabric with the smaller template. Before folding the margins over and basting them in place, clip any corners or curves up to the drawn outline as shown.

Fig. 207. An appliqué of pattern II-4, in royal blue and black on a white ground. The shapes are enlarged to the size indicated in Fig. 208. The outlines of the design were transferred to the foundation fabric by direct tracing, shifting the drawing as necessary. The cut and basted shapes are to be applied with a blind hemming stitch.

181

Transferring a Design to Fabric

First you need the design drawn actual size on a sheet of tracing paper laid over the pattern sheet. If the entire design does not fit on the pattern sheet because the shapes have been enlarged, be sure to include at least one repeat in the tracing (Fig. 208). Even if the design has not been enlarged, it is likely that the area to be covered on the foundation fabric will be greater than the area of the pattern sheet; so, in either case, you will have to shift the tracing along the fabric to transfer the entire design. The many lines of the design itself will serve as accurate registration points. To transfer the design from the tracing paper to fabric, use one of the following three methods.

1. *Direct Tracing*. If the fabric is light, and thin enough to see through when held up to the light, you can place the fabric over the tracing, hold both up to daylight and copy the lines directly. First tape the traced drawing to a window pane; then tape the fabric over it. Trace the design in pencil. (Any pencil marks which are visible after the shapes are sewn can be lightly erased, or can be washed out when the piece is finished.) Reposition the fabric over the tracing as often as necessary to repeat the desired outlines until you have extended the design to the proper dimensions.

2. *Back Tracing*. On the reverse side of the traced drawing, go over each line with a soft pencil. Place the drawing reverse side down on the fabric and tape or pin it into place. Retrace each line on the right side of the drawing with a sharp pencil or a stylus. The soft pencil lines on the reverse side will appear on the fabric. (If the fabric is dark, use chalk rather than soft pencil to go over the lines on the back of the tracing.)

Fig. 208. Draw the design to its actual size. If the entire design does not fit on the pattern sheet, include one repeat of the motif. This traced portion can be shifted along the fabric to transfer the entire design.

3. *Carbon Paper.* Use dressmaker's carbon paper. This comes in light colors for marking dark fabrics, and dark colors for marking light fabrics. Tape the fabric to a flat surface. Place the carbon paper face down on it, and then tape the traced drawing into place over the carbon paper. Go over all the lines of the design carefully, with a pencil, stylus, or tracing wheel.

Quilting

When a piece of patchwork or appliqué is made into a quilt, running stitches, called quilting, must be sewn through three layers of cloth: the decorated top, the interlining (batting), and the backing. These stitches hold the quilt in shape and keep the interlining from bunching up. In addition to its practical use, however, quilting can form a separate, decorative pattern which either reiterates or complements the design. In fact, if there is no decoration on the top layer, the quilting stitches themselves can form a beautiful design (Fig. 209). All the designs given in this book can be adapted as quilting patterns. The design can first be transferred to the fabric as described in the preceding paragraphs.

Fig. 209. The overlapping circles of pattern sheet IV, with diagonal lines, form the central motif in this decoratively quilted, wool coverlet. (American textiles, ca. 1750; The Metropolitan Museum of Art, Rogers Fund, 1945.)

Materials for Patchwork and Appliqué

Despite the philosophical origin of patchwork, it is always better to use new rather than used fabric. It will wear better and be easier to work with. I recommend a firmly woven cloth that will not fray, such as strong, lightweight cotton. Also good are linen, flannel, chintz, silk, satin and velvet. (Velvet is a bit more difficult to work with, but many fine, Victorian patchworks were done in combinations of silk and velvet or satin and velvet.) Unbleached muslin is serviceable for the foundation fabric of an appliqué design, or as a backing for an entire piece (for instance, a quilt). Felt is often used for appliqué, since the edges remain clean when cut. In general, I've found that natural rather than synthetic fabrics work best.

Materials should be preshrunk and colorfast. Best effects are achieved by working the same kinds of fabrics together in one piece. Never combine washable and unwashable fabrics such as cotton and silk.

In general, either mercerized cotton or silk sewing thread is best, depending upon the fabric you are working with. A single strand of embroidery thread also works well. To appliqué with a decorative embroidery stitch, use cotton or silk embroidery thread. Thread coated with silicone works best for quilting.

Patchwork Patterns

The patterns which follow are designed expressly for patchwork. For the most part they are patterns which, like Fig. 212 use large shapes that span many units on the pattern sheet. In Fig. 212, two large motifs (Figs. 210 and 211) are combined and repeated to make a very large quilt for a double bed. When the piece was quilted, large squares were sewn within the large diamond shapes to make an interesting counter-pattern.

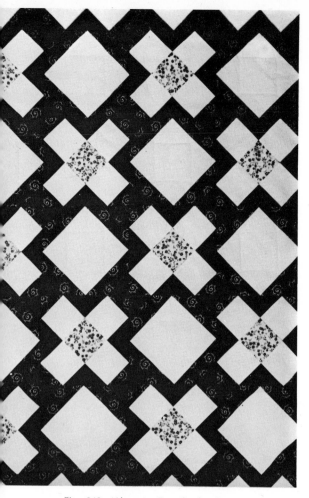

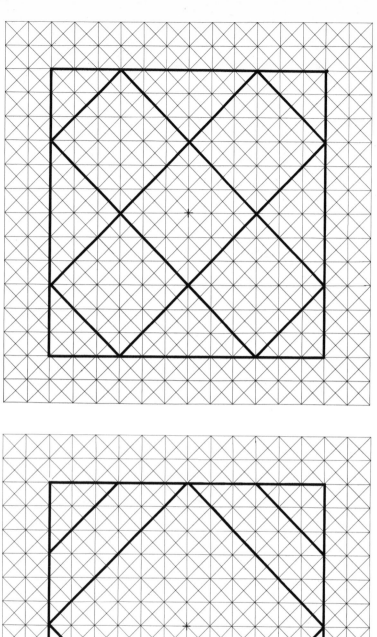

Fig. 212. (Above) Detail of a large patchwork quilt by Beth Gutcheon. Called "Greenberg Bride's Quilt," it is worked in cotton fabric. The colors are white, dark green, and dark red, with a light green-and-red floral print. Quilting was added within the large, white diamond shapes.

Fig. 210. (Upper right) Pattern for one block of "Greenberg Bride's Quilt." See detail above.

Fig. 211. (Lower right) Pattern for second block of the same quilt.

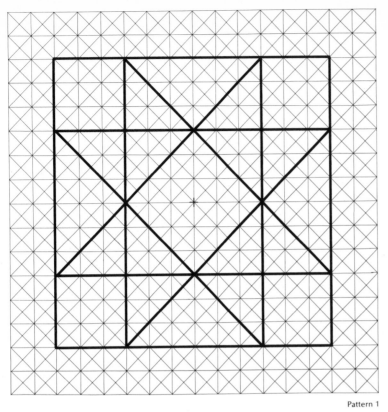

Pattern 1

Pattern 1 shows how the needlepoint designs in previous chapters can be adapted to patchwork. It is an enlargement of the eight-pointed star motif of pattern I-9 (page 56). Each line was originally one unit long on the pattern sheet and is now three units long. The motif is separated by bands of a contrasting color in the patchwork shown (Fig. 213).

Fig. 213. Design for a scrap quilt by Marcia Schonzeit. Many different, printed fabrics are used for the eight-pointed stars, which are surrounded by solid-color fabrics. (See color page 164.)

Pattern 2

Pattern 2 is pattern II-20 (page 95) doubled in scale for patchwork. The same procedure can be used with most patterns based on pattern sheet I, II, or III with equally satisfying results.

Fig. 214. Patchwork pillow by Winifred Bendiner, made with silk fabric. The printed areas are parts of old neckties, and the entire design is mounted on velvet. (See color page 164.)

Pattern 2

Pattern 3

Pattern 3, composed of octagons and diamonds, is often seen in floor-tile designs. The same configuration, hidden or embellished upon, appears in some of the octagonal designs based on pattern sheet II. Enlarged, as in this line drawing, these shapes make an easy-to-handle patchwork pattern with many charming possibilities. One would be to color four octagons similarly, forming a near-square block. The diamond in the center could be of a dark solid color, with the eight surrounding diamonds being brightly colored.

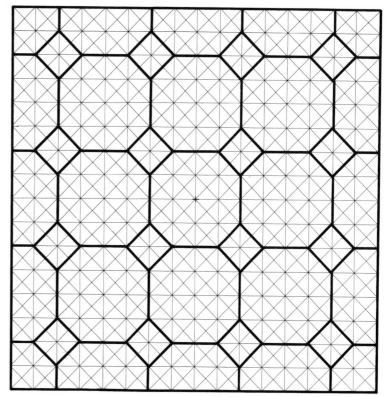

Pattern 3

Pattern 4

Pattern 4 is a diamond pattern that appears in many famous masterpiece quilts. It is called by various names: Harvest Sun, Star of Bethlehem, Star of the West, Rising Sun, and others. It is extended from the center to produce ever-larger eight-pointed stars by adding more diamond shapes (the center star and the first ring of added diamond shapes are shown in the line drawing to illustrate the principle). Often it is colored with the center star light, and each succeeding ring slightly darker, to approximate the feeling of a shining star.

Pattern 5

The eight-pointed stars of pattern 5 are constructed in the same way as the center star of the preceding design. Here, however, the stars are separated by large squares and right-angled diamonds. The three elements of this design are numbered on the drawing. They are the (1) obtuse-angled diamond (rhombus), (2) the right-angled diamond, and (3) the large square. One good way to color this design is to make all the squares the same or a similar dark color, and all the stars light. The total design will then look like a network of stars strung out against a dark night sky. (Perfect for a quilt, wouldn't you say?)

Pattern 6

The design of pattern 6, while it may bear a visual resemblance to pattern 4, is actually quite different structurally. For one thing, it is based upon a six-pointed star rather than one that has eight points. For another, it is drawn on pattern sheet III rather than pattern sheet II.

To make this pattern, you need cut only one shape: the diamond. The larger shapes are made by sewing diamonds together; the six-pointed star has six diamonds, the chevron shape has two (Fig. 215). The shapes are sewn together as pictured to form a large hexagon. This hexagon is then sewn to other identically constructed hexagons (hexagons of the same size fit together exactly).

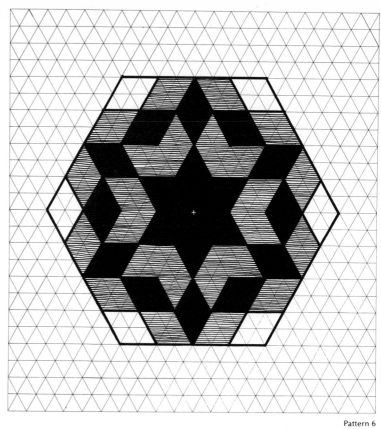

Pattern 6

Fig. 215. Only one shape is required to piece together this pattern.

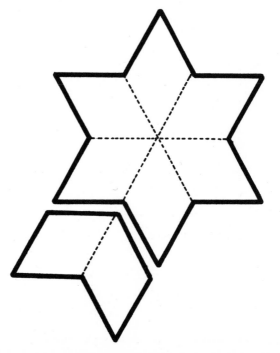

189

Pattern 7

Pattern 7

Pattern 7 can be worked equally well, in the size it is given, as a patchwork or as a needlepoint design. Fig. 216 shows how it can be colored to achieve a three-dimensional effect, like a panel of cubby-holes set on end.

When working this pattern in patchwork, the narrow bands which run through the design must be pieced. How this is done is shown by the dotted lines on the line drawing; the bands are broken up into small squares and rectangles. The templates you will need are numbered. They are: (1) a right-angled diamond, which is actually a square set on end; (2) a trapezoid; and (3) the rectangle and small square (4) which make up the crossing bands.

Fig. 216. Pattern can be colored to achieve three-dimensional effect.

Pattern 8

This design and those which follow have their origin in the characteristically American patchwork tradition. Their common denominator is that a repeat of the design is encompassed within a square block. The blocks are sewn into long strips, which are then sewn together side to side. This procedure makes assembly of the patchwork very easy, once the proper number of blocks have been made.

The basic octagon combined with triangles at its corners forms the square shown in pattern 8, which was repeated to create the patchwork shown in Fig. 217. By keeping the corner triangles of each square the same light color, a background is established which creates quite a different figure in the combined pattern than is apparent in a single repeat.

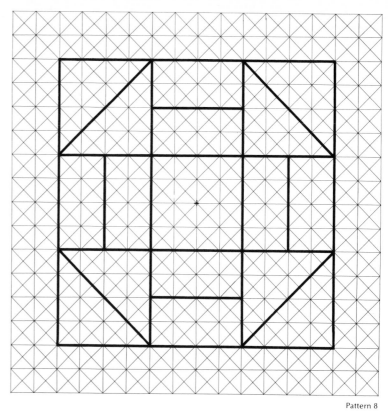

Pattern 8

Fig. 217. Baby's coverlet by Florence Youree, made with cotton and chintz fabric. (See color page 159.)

191

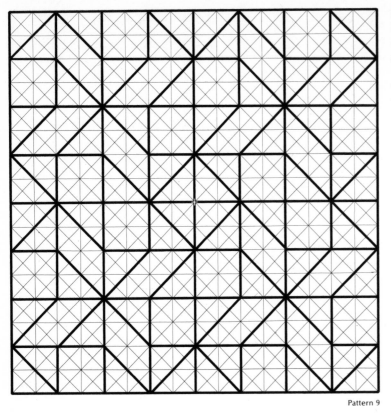

Pattern 9

Pattern 9

Pattern 9 is called "Jeffrey's Choice," after its creator, Jeffrey Gutcheon. It is a variation on a traditional patchwork pattern known as "Clay's Choice" (which dates from a time when Henry Clay was a prominent political figure in this country). Four repeats are shown, each occupying one-quarter of the line drawing (8 by 8 units).

Fig. 218. (Opposite page) Patchwork quilt by Jeffrey Gutcheon, measuring approximately 34 by 42 inches. Printed and solid-color fabrics were carefully chosen and combined to create the dark and light counter-pattern in this design. (See color page 159.)

Pattern 10

Pattern 10

Pattern 10 is called "Corn and Beans," illustrating the whimsical and totally arbitrary nature of some patchwork names. (If a design doesn't look like something, you can call it anything—a principle which was followed in patchwork long before modern art came along.) It is worked by sewing ten small triangles together with two large ones to form each square block of 6 by 6 units. The dotted lines indicate how to piece the triangles.

Pattern 11

Although pattern 11 has been called "Monkey's Wrench" or "Snail's Tail," you may think of other names when working it. The progression of diminishing triangles, each of which fits so precisely with its counterparts to form a square, has a kind of satisfying mathematical inevitability. The dark and light spirals that are formed (Fig. 219) are like a patchwork version of the Chinese yin-yang principle. The pattern can be worked in either appliqué or patchwork. For appliqué, sew dark triangles to a light square, making two opposing spirals. For patchwork, piece each triangle forming the spirals as indicated by the dotted lines in the upper-right quarter of the line drawing.

Fig. 219. Pattern colored as light and dark spirals.

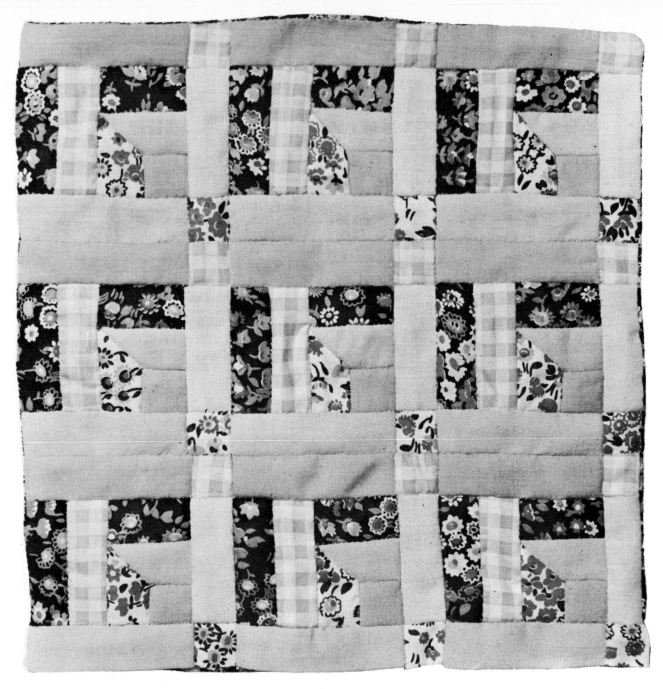

Fig. 220. An original patchwork pillow casing, by Carol DiSepio; it measures 15 by 15 inches. The small squares are one-inch in each direction, and every other shape in the design measures one inch in either its height or its width.

11. Designing Your Own Pattern

One of the very unique features of the pattern sheets included with this book is that they allow you to become a "pattern designer" on your own. The pattern sheets provide a counted-stitch structure of geometric shapes upon which to draw original designs. Once you have created a design, you will know how many stitches are required for each shape, and exactly where to place the stitches on your canvas.

I recommend that you try this creative and rewarding aspect of pattern design only after you have completed some of the given designs and have become experienced in working with the pattern sheets. While working, you will discover the principles of pattern design, and the many examples in this book will provide the inspiration and the visual information you will need to create designs of your own.

Nowadays many artists, not only needlecrafters, are returning to basic geometric principles. Geometry provides a structure and a point of departure for finding one's own, personal direction. It is perhaps paradoxical, but true, that having a structure from which to build allows one to create even more freely than would otherwise be possible. The given structure eliminates unnecessary preliminaries and enables you to immediately make those choices of taste that are the heart of creating a personal design. And, in my experience, it is more gratifying to work your own design in needlepoint (or patchwork), since it is so uniquely your own. Some basic approaches to creating original designs are described in the following paragraphs.

1. *Using the pattern sheet itself as a design.* Many handsome and interesting designs can be developed by keeping to the root shapes of a pattern sheet and creating your design through a network of beautiful color changes. The linear clarity of these "root" patterns provides a much wider latitude for color experimentation than would be possible with more complex designs. You may vary the sizes of the root shapes (doubling or tripling them as for patchwork), or you may make some other, simple linear variation. Those familiar with modern art will recognize this principle as one used by many contemporary artists.

A variation of this idea is to use the entire pattern sheet as a background, combining it with another shape or design used as the central motif. The central motif can be one of your own invention, or it can be one of the given designs, which you put into this new context.

2. *Combining given designs.* The idea people have of what is "good taste" is constantly changing. It is no longer taboo, for example, to combine two or more autonomous patterns in one design. These designs may be adjacent, in a concentric formation, or combined (see color plates 4 and 19). This concept is especially useful for large pieces of work.

When combining given designs, it is best to restrict oneself to designs from a single chapter, since each pattern sheet has its own sequence of stitches. Designs based on pattern sheets II and IV are an exception, as the stitches of each one will combine evenly with the other. If you combine designs based on the other pattern sheets, you must compensate for the variation in the number of stitches by adding extra rows where needed, unless you wish to simply let the shapes fall where they may.

3. *Drawing freely over the pattern sheet.* The process of freely drawing designs over the lines of the pattern sheet is one which I never fail to find absorbing. The only rule is to follow the lines of the pattern sheet, and the object is to create a coherent and good-looking design.

Start by placing a sheet of tracing paper over the pattern sheet. The next step is to look hard at the crossing network of lines, and simply let shapes and forms drift to the surface of your consciousness. Trace the forms that most strike your fancy; you will probably draw tentatively at first and then with increasing sureness as a design begins to emerge. You may find yourself making a picture, or a rhythmic pattern design. In either case, follow the impulse to wherever it leads. Perhaps you will make a false start and have to discard a sheet of tracing paper. No matter; the ideas which were incomplete at first may be brought to fruition on the second or third try.

Many surprising forms lie dormant within the lines of each pattern sheet, waiting to be discovered and put to use. The curved lines of pattern sheet IV lend themselves especially well to this process (see patterns IV-13, 19, 20, and 21, all original designs made in this way).

I have learned, through the research I did to find the patterns presented here, that the process of making designs upon a geometric network is an ever-changing one. A pattern may first appear in Greek ornament and resurface hundreds of years later in the Near East completely transformed, while in the Orient the same pattern is being developed along parallel but different lines. This indicates to me a living, organic process of growth and change. People everywhere take the designs that history presents to them and subtly change them to conform to their likes and needs. I hope that this book in its own way will help the reader to participate in that process.